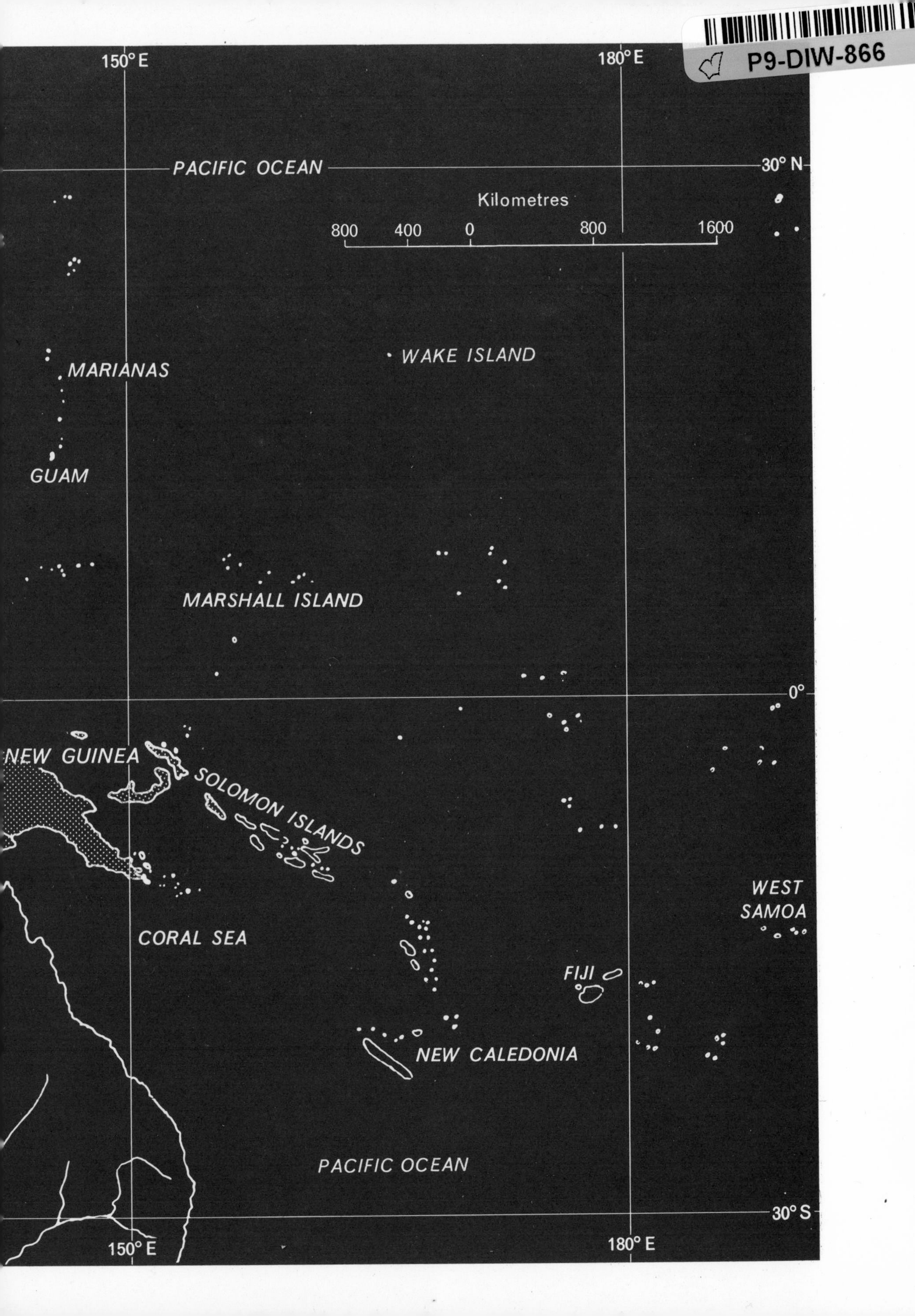
150° E
180° E
PACIFIC OCEAN
30° N
Kilometres
800 400 0 800 1600
WAKE ISLAND
MARIANAS
GUAM
MARSHALL ISLAND
0°
NEW GUINEA
SOLOMON ISLANDS
CORAL SEA
WEST SAMOA
FIJI
NEW CALEDONIA
PACIFIC OCEAN
30° S
150° E
180° E

Shells of New Guinea
and the
Central Indo-Pacific

For John Mark Huston, conchologist, at Christmas Time, 1975, with love from his Father

Shells of New Guinea and the Central Indo-Pacific

A. G. Hinton

with colour photographs by the author

Robert Brown and Associates Pty Ltd
The Jacaranda Press

First published 1972 jointly by
ROBERT BROWN AND ASSOCIATES PTY LTD
P.O. Box 3395, Port Moresby, P.N.G.
and
JACARANDA PRESS PTY LTD
65 Park Road, Milton, Q.
20 Falcon Street, Crows Nest, N.S.W.
37 Little Bourke Street, Melbourne, Vic.
142 Colin Street, West Perth, W.A.
303 Wright Street, Adelaide, S.A.
57 France Street, Auckland, N.Z.
P.O. Box 3395, Port Moresby, P.N.G.
70A Greenleaf Road, Singapore 10

Typesetting by Queensland Type Service Pty Ltd
Printed in Hong Kong

Reprinted in Hong Kong 1975

National Library of Australia
Card Number and ISBN 0 7016 8114 4

Contents

Foreword

There is no area that has a richer fauna than the Central Indo-Pacific. New Guinea lies well within this region and thus living in New Guinea Alan Hinton is well placed to become thoroughly acquainted with the multitude of species at his back door.

Most of the world's major museums, and therefore most of the professional malacologists, are situated well away from tropical seas. Partly because of this the tropical Indo-Pacific fauna has been sadly neglected by malacologists.

However, this lack of professional activity has been more than compensated for by the tremendous enthusiasm and prodigious activities of shell collectors, observers, photographers and naturalists. The extravagant colour and form produced in many tropical species have captivated many a casual observer and turned some into serious amateur conchologists whose special knowledge often surpasses that of the museum specialists.

Alan Hinton has specialized in the very large family Conidae and is an authority on the Central Indo-Pacific species. Living amongst them he has a considerable knowledge of their ecology, feeding behaviour and variability. Unfortunately space has not permitted him a greater opportunity to place on record much of the valuable data that he has accumulated.

This book is primarily designed to aid shell collectors in identifying their specimens and the superb colour photographs should make species recognition a simple matter. Some of the names used will be unavoidably changed over the next few years but this will not be a reflection on the efforts of Alan Hinton but on the generally unstable state of molluscan systematics.

Whereas numerous books are available to collectors concerned with temperate faunas the Indo-Pacific species are, for the most part, almost impossible to identify unless a comprehensive library of molluscan literature is available. Because many of the very necessary books and journals are extremely rare and expensive such libraries are few and far between. There is thus an urgent necessity for books on this fauna so that identification can become a relatively simple matter for amateur and professional alike.

Winston F. Ponder
Curator of Molluscs
The Australian Museum Sydney

Acknowledgments

The author gratefully acknowledges the technical assistance and information so generously given by a number of people, in the preparation of the text for this handbook. I am particularly indebted to Dr W. F. Ponder and Mr P. Colman of the Australian Museum, Mr W. E. Old junior of the American Museum of Natural History, Dr A. J. Kohn of the University of Washington, Mr W. O. Cernohorsky of the Auckland Institute and Museum, Mr W. G. Krause of Avoca Beach, New South Wales and Mr Hal Lewis of Wynewood, Pa.
For the loan of specimens and accompanying data, my thanks to Marg and Fred Kleckham (*Cypraea guttata*), Ann and Keith McCollim, Geoff Harvey, Joyce and Don Murray, Ed Petuch and Roger Buick. For constructive criticism and suggestions I thank my many friends, and fellow members of the Port Moresby branch of the Malacological Society of Australia. And finally I thank my wife and family for their patience and understanding during the many months our home was cluttered with papers, shells and photographic paraphernalia.

Introduction

Man has always collected shells. For those with a yen to collect, few products of nature can rival the beauty of the glossy texture, showy colour or exquisite form of sea shells.

The inhabitants of the countless islands scattered over the tropical waters of the Central Indo-Pacific were among the earliest shell collectors. Excavations reveal layer upon layer of accumulated shell deposits, dating centuries before history was recorded. Archaeologists rely to a large extent on durable shell material in attempts to solve the mysteries of ancient cultures, civilizations, and population migrations. Although molluscs were collected primarily for food, as evidenced by the vast quantities of shells found on present and old village sites, many species were collected for other purposes. Larger specimens were adapted for such practical uses as utensils for carrying and holding food and water, bailing dug-out canoes, and for fashioning cutting edges and arrow and spear heads. Others attained symbolic status and became part of the culture of primitive island people, being worn as charms or as an indication of wealth, rank or station. Some were planted in gardens to ensure a bountiful crop, others decorated canoes as good luck charms. Shells were, and still are, worn extensively for body adornment. In many of the remote island groups of the Pacific, sea shells are still used as a trade medium and as a form of currency.

Today, shell collecting is a hobby enjoyed by people of all countries and from all walks of life. The healthy outdoor activity of beach and reef fossicking, the excitement of adding new forms to a growing collection, and pride of an attractive display cabinet and the aesthetic interest and challenge in the identification and scientific classification of specimens, combine to make this hobby a most rewarding and relaxing pastime.

This colour-illustrated handbook is devised for two purposes: firstly, to assist the collector in identifying shells from this area, and secondly, to include as many of the species variations occasioned by range and distribution, and by variation in colour and form between juveniles and adults, as space permits. Regrettably, the space and relative cost limitations imposed on any such undertaking as this will allow the illustration of only the most popular families of shells.

To permit ready reference to the specimen illustrated, the text, including name and brief commentary, is printed on the facing page. With some deviation necessitated by the problem of photographing specimens of various sizes on the one plate, the shells appear in the currently accepted systematic order. Subgeneric and subspecific names have been omitted in most cases, as they are considered unnecessary to the average collector and are constantly under review. Variations of the one species are listed as forms. Further study of these shells may cause some to be elevated to specific ranking, and likewise other currently accepted species to be found synonymous. Where possible, obviously related or similar species are illustrated together to simplify identification.

The Mollusc

The animal kingdom is divided into a number of major groups called phyla.

The Phylum Mollusca includes a group of soft-bodied animals which have, in most cases, a hard external skeletal covering known as a *shell.* This phylum is further divided into seven classes: Monoplacophora, Aplacophora, Polyplacophora (chitons), Gastropoda, Bivalvia (bivalves), Scaphopoda (tusk shells), and Cephalopoda.

Only the spirally coiled snail-like molluscs of the Class Gastropoda are dealt with in this handbook. They are mostly colourful and showy, and are natural favourites with amateur collectors. Other gastropods include slugs, limpets, and sea butterflies (Pteropoda).

Most of the members of the Class Cephalopoda have lost their external shells, and include the squids, cuttlefishes and octopuses. One that has retained a shell is the pearly nautilus.

To the layman, the barnacles superficially resemble molluscs, but are actually related to the crabs, prawns etc., and placed under the Phylum Arthropoda. Another group often confused with bivalve molluscs is the brachiopoda, a distinct phylum which differs in actually having an internal skeletal structure or lophophore.

On the other hand, the worm-like teredo worms which bore into wooden piles and ships' hulls are true bivalve molluscs.

New Guinea

Recognized as one of the largest islands in the world, New Guinea lies entirely in the tropics, and is geographically situated in the centre of the Indo-Pacific Province. The western part of the island is now part of greater Indonesia, and the eastern section, including the larger islands of New Britain, New Ireland and Bougainville, with hundreds of smaller islands often forming island chains or archipelagoes, was administered by the Commonwealth of Australia until 1 December 1973. The former Trust Territory of New Guinea and the former Australian possession of Papua are now united as Papua New Guinea, which will be fully independent by the end of 1975.

The highlands of New Guinea, which extend the entire length of the island, are a spectacular series of folds created in recent geological times, and rise to heights in excess of 4,500 metres, and a lush impenetrable jungle covers most of the terrain. An unstable line extends roughly along the northern coastline, with active volcanoes offshore and on the larger islands of New Britain, New Ireland and Bougainville.

With the exception of the Sepik and Ramu River estuaries, most of the northern coastline of New Guinea drops suddenly to great ocean depths, with a rugged foreshore and rocky headlands, and with only brief patches of fringing coral reef. The harshness of the shoreline is broken by several well-protected bays and harbours. Scattered offshore are volcanic peaks rising like cones from the ocean. The lofty peaks of New Britain can be seen from the mainland on a clear day, but the intervening ocean is over a thousand fathoms deep.

In eastern Papua, an outer barrier reef protects the main shoreline and forms a comparatively shallow coastal strip of water studded with coral reefs and small islands.

The Fly River and numerous lesser rivers pour a continuous stream of dirty water into the Gulf of Papua. These shallow turbid waters of the gulf are devoid of coral reefs, and the shoreline is fringed with mangrove swamps.

Some of the island chains off eastern Papua, such as the Louisiade Archipelago and the Lusancay and Trobriand Island Groups, comprise numerous large and small islands and sand cays, and thousands of square miles of shallow water and luxuriant coral reefs.

The Central Indo-Pacific

The tropical geographical situation and the diversity of suitable environmental conditions are responsible for the rich and varied molluscan fauna which New Guinea shares with north-east Australia, the innumerable islands north-west and north towards Japan, and the island groups eastward to Fiji and Samoa. Under these circumstances, it is not surprising to discover that New Guinea is the centre of distribution of many species of shells, and some species, rare elsewhere, are more abundant in these waters. The molluscan fauna is typically Indo-Pacific, and most species occurring over this vast province are to be found in some form along the New Guinea shorelines.

In recent years, deepwater dredging and trawling have shown that a north-south distributional pattern occurs, extending roughly from Japan to south Queensland. For instance species of cowries, cones, epitoniums and several other shells, dredged from deep water along the east coast of Australia, were, until very recently, known only from the China Sea. In some cases these shells have not been taken in the intervening seas, but commercial trawling operations have been minimal over much of this area. It is reasonable to assume that in some if not all instances, they do occur over the entire range, at variable depths according to the ecological requirements of the individual species.

In the ensuing text and illustrations, it will be noted that most of the featured specimens were collected in New Guinea. However, some divergence from a fully restricted selection is also evident. An attempt has been made to include variations and forms occurring within the rather flexible and vague boundaries of the "Central Indo-Pacific" — Japan southwards to north Australia, and from south-east Asia and the islands of Indonesia eastwards to Fiji.

Collecting for the Beginner

Shells are so abundant in the reef-fringed islands of the tropical seas that each rising tide deposits a new layer of shells upon the accumulation of the past, and many beaches comprise shells and shell fragments rather than sand. Occasionally an unusual find may be made by merely fossicking through the beach debris, particularly after a period of high winds and rough seas, but generally, beach collected specimens are of poor quality and lack the lustre, colour and sculpture definition of live shells. However, a brief study of this material is a handy guide to the quantity and type of shells living in the area.

Whether walking on exposed reef at low tide, wading with a viewing window, swimming and snorkelling or dredging, shell collecting on tropical coral reefs is thrilling, exhilarating and rewarding. Many curious sightseers and casual swimmers have become amateur naturalists and fanatic collectors after their first excursion. To observe the behaviour pattern of the multitude of colourful marine creatures in their natural environment is a wondrous sight and an educational experience.

When collecting on a coral reef, or swimming near coral, a few precautions may save the novice much pain and discomfort. The newcomer from cooler climes is, for some inexplicable reason, more susceptible to the minor irritant poisons of echinoderms (spiny sea-urchins), some soft and semi-soft corals, sea anemones and other marine life, which abound in tropical waters. In time this susceptibility wanes, and the effects of these irritant stings are very temporary and easily endured. Coral cuts and abrasions can be painful and easily become infected. Light but complete body encasing clothing is advisable when reef collecting, and protective footwear and heavy gloves are essential. The dangers of handling poisonous cone shells are dealt with fully under the introduction to the family Conidae.

The shells that live above the tide lines, usually on rocky foreshores, and often in colonies, are interesting biologically, but lack the size and colour of their neighbours in the littoral zone, and are often neglected by collectors.

The littoral or intertidal zone supports a large and varied population of shells. In a locality with a gradually sloping shoreline, and wide tidal variations, the area of exposed reefs or beach flats is very extensive at low tide. This is the area most readily accessible to and favoured by collectors. Some sand-dwelling shells leave a well-defined track, and bury themselves during day-light hours. Early in the morning, or at night with lights, as the tide begins to rise, is the best time to collect terebras, cassids, naticids and other sand dwellers. Cowries, cones, murex and cymatiids hide under stones, coral, weed patches and in crevices. When turning stone or coral boulders in search of these shells, always replace the boulders to preserve the molluscs' natural habitat.

Below the tide levels, shell collecting is restricted to the more daring and energetic enthusiasts. Swimming with snorkel or aqualung is an interesting and exciting method of collecting. The shallow sandy lagoons and patches between coral and rock outcrops are usually rich in molluscs. In such areas where the water is from waist to shoulder deep, just below the low tide level, collecting is both rewarding and enjoyable. Wearing mask, snorkel and flippers, it is possible to collect for some hours without tiring. Fanning the sand bottom with a flipper will expose the colourful terebras, sand cones, naticidae and other species. A calico or heavy cloth bag attached to a belt will allow for greater comfort and manoeuvrability when swimming.

The molluscs that live below the tidal influence are generally scarce, as they are less accessible to collectors. Dredging is the only practical way to collect live specimens. The design, size, and weight of the dredge depends on the power and other facilities of the towing unit. A small cage-like scoop can be towed by an outboard-powered dinghy and retrieved by hand, but the larger dredges which are proportionately more efficient, require a winch to handle the weight and to make a quick recovery from the depths. Enquire from field collectors associated with natural history museums and similar institutions on the most suitable and efficient type of dredges.

Prawn trawlermen and scallop dredgers supply dealers with quantities of shells, and these commercial operators cause seasonal fluctuations in the availability of shell specimens. Some years ago the first prawn trawlers dredged an amazing assortment of shells from the prawn beds close inshore and in localities in easy reach of safe ports and catch-handling depots. As prawn stocks became depleted, the fishermen worked deeper waters along the continental shelves, and larger vessels were constructed that could remain at sea for longer periods. Still new shell finds were made and many new species named. This development occurred world-wide during the past fifteen to twenty years, a rich and bountiful period for both the collector and the student of malacology. Alas, more recently, streamlining techniques have been introduced in the pattern of nets and the method of dredging whereby the commercial trawlers can by-pass rubbish and bottom sediment, saving the fishermen's valuable time in separating the prawn catch. Already this trend is evident in some areas where trawlermen are the only source of supply of live-collected material. The supply is visibly dwindling, and species available a few years ago are becoming scarce and costly to procure.

Exchanging specimens with collectors in other areas will help to expand your collection and permit a comparative study of range variations of many species. The formation of clubs has permitted an interchange of ideas and observations, and an exchange of specimens undreamed of a few years ago.

Reputable dealers issue price lists from time to time on request, and in this manner many foreign specimens can be procured at a reasonable cost.

Classification and Display

The world's leading conchologists disagree on the taxonomy of many shells, so the collector has problems when identifying and labelling his specimens. The professionals in this challenging field of science are usually domiciled in the larger cities and in research institutions of the more advanced lands where equipment and comprehensive reference material are available. These experts, for the greater part of their research programmes, must rely on material sent to them from all parts of the globe. Naturally, this material is often inadequate as the animal which is so necessary to determine relationships accurately is not easily transportable. Even today, much of molluscan taxonomy is based merely on shell characteristics. Surprisingly, this applies to many of the more common species as well as the rarer ones. The collector finds his cabinet featuring shell specimens from various localities with different names, but obviously closely related one with another. In some cases they are the same species. In other instances, some species vary so considerably over a range, that specimens from extremities of the range differ greatly in colour, form and even sculpture. In such cases a series of intergrading forms is necessary to show that they are the one species. The mass of synonymy resulting from varietal forms over the vast range of the Indo-Pacific, causes such confusion among today's collectors that many justifiably lose interest through frustration. With the recent upsurge in interest in shell collecting, many of the hitherto rarer species are becoming available to scientists and a greater understanding is now possible of the life cycle, distribution and species to species relationship (generic grouping) of many shells.

If data is recorded for each live collected specimen, the correct classification and specific name is of secondary importance. Naturally, a keen collector is anxious to have his shells correctly named, as this creates an added interest and challenge in acquiring a comprehensive collection. However, the name can be settled at a later date by scrutinizing literature or by referring the doubtful specimen to a recognized authority, but, if left to memory, the locality, observations of circumstances and conditions of collection become doubtful and even misleading.

The amateur collector in the field can be of invaluable assistance to the taxonomist by retaining, where possible, the shell preserved in its natural condition. When preserved in 70 per cent alcohol, the specimen may be held indefinitely with no damage to even the most delicate or lustrous shell. In alcohol the animal will harden in time, and formalin is preferable for preserving the soft animal tissues for future study. However, formalin will cause acidic corrosion of delicate shells unless neutralized by saturating the formalin with an alkali such as baking soda or borax. Three teaspoons of baking soda in $2\frac{1}{4}$ litres of concentrated or raw formalin is adequate. Ten per cent neutralized formalin in a formalin and salt water solution is an ideal preservative.

The system of cataloguing and naming shells is dependent on the individual's requirements, available spare time and his degree of scientific interest. The simplest method is to record each specimen or series in a catalogue with a sequence number. This reference number may be attached to the specimen by printing the number directly on to the shell, on a card inserted in the shell, or enclosed in the box, phial, or plastic bag as applicable. In well-catalogued collections, the entry should include at least the genus, the specific name, the authority, such pertinent data as locality and habitat of the specimen(s), the date and any other interesting information on abundance and behaviour. e.g.:

Cypraea tigris Linne. Near low tide mark under algae-covered coral debris on protected inner reef, Port Moresby Harbour, on 14 March, 1970. (Collector — J. Doe). Numerous bulla stage juveniles noted in vicinity.

The display of specimens is another matter, adaptable to the individual's taste and interest, and it depends on finance and room for storage or display. Some collections, arranged in glass fronted cabinets with mirror backs and artificial lighting, are a glory to behold, and can be used to highlight the interior decor of a home. Other collectors prefer closed cabinets with drawers to prevent the penetration of light that does, in time, cause fading of colourful and glossy specimens. Matchboxes, cardboard and cigar boxes, glass phials and self-sealing plastic bags are all excellent storing receptacles that ensure that indentification tags are not lost.

Where applicable, the operculum should be retained with each specimen, and if the specimen has an epidermis, or outer skin covering, it is advisable to describe this before dressing the shell for cabinet display or storage. Museums and some serious collectors retain a "wet collection" or series of preserved specimens of as many species as practicable.

A salt water aquarium is a fascinating way of observing marine molluscs. It can be arranged in an attractive and decorative manner.

Cleaning Shells

Removing the animal from sea shells can be tedious, but the time and effort spent on this task is both necessary and worthwhile to prevent the unpleasant smell of decomposition and the attraction of flies and other insects.

Only collect shells you require for your collection, and perhaps a few specimens suitable for exchanges. The collector who cannot resist keeping every pretty shell he sights will invariably waste many of them as he will not be able to cope with the cleaning operation. The collection of a few choice specimens of each species will not interfere with a shell population, but indiscriminate and wasteful collecting will.

Cleaning shells while they are still fresh is not an unpleasant and smelly task. The exercise can be likened to opening edible oysters, scallops or abalones, or cleaning fish, and there should be no aversion to doing the work in the comfort of the kitchen. Shells may be boiled to facilitate cleaning with no damage or loss of natural sheen, providing they are brought to the boil slowly, allowed to simmer gently for ten to fifteen minutes, then cooled gradually. Sudden temperature changes will fracture the nacreous surface of shells. If it is not convenient to clean the specimens immediately after collection, they can be washed to remove slime and mud, and placed in a plastic container in the refrigerator or deep-freeze. This will not harm them in any way. Should refrigeration space not be available, shells can be held in 70 per cent alcohol or methylated spirit, and the animal removed when time permits. If left in alcohol for more than a few days, the mollusc tends to harden, but will soften with boiling, and there is no unpleasant smell. An assortment of wire hooks, pins, and tweezers is ideal for the task and, with patience, the animal can be removed from most shells. If there is any possibility of some of the soft tissue remaining within the coils of the shell, place the shell in alcohol for a couple of weeks, then dry in a shady place free of insects, and plug the aperture with cotton wool. Very small shells and certain larger forms have a very narrow aperture, and removal of the animal is impossible. These specimens are best preserved for some weeks in alcohol, dried, and plugged with cotton wool. Some collectors are content to allow the soft tissues to rot away in sand or water rather than persevere with hand cleaning. This method is satisfactory for those shells which are protected with a coarse epidermis during the period of decomposition, but cowries, olives and volutes tend to develop dull patches and a general loss of their natural sheen.

Some gastropods possess an operculum which is either horny or calcareous. This should be retained with the shell, as serious collectors will not accept in exchanges specimens that are missing this item. The operculum is helpful in classifying shells, as the members of each group or genus, and in some cases whole families, have opercula with similar structure and basic characteristics. The presence of the operculum is also an assurance that the specimen was collected live.

Cone shells, cymatiids and several other families of shells possess an epidermis or periostracum (outer skin) when alive. This periostracum is often useful in distinguishing species, so that at least some specimens should be retained intact. However, the periostracum can be removed by soaking in a concentrated household bleach. The bleach will also soften and facilitate the removal of coralline and other foreign matter.

Abrasive polishing and acid treatment of shells is not countenanced by serious collectors, but a little oil to restore the surface sheen after the drying-out processes of preserving and bleaching is quite acceptable.

Whatever cleaning method is adopted, refrain from exposing shell specimens to strong sunlight as this will cause them to fade rapidly.

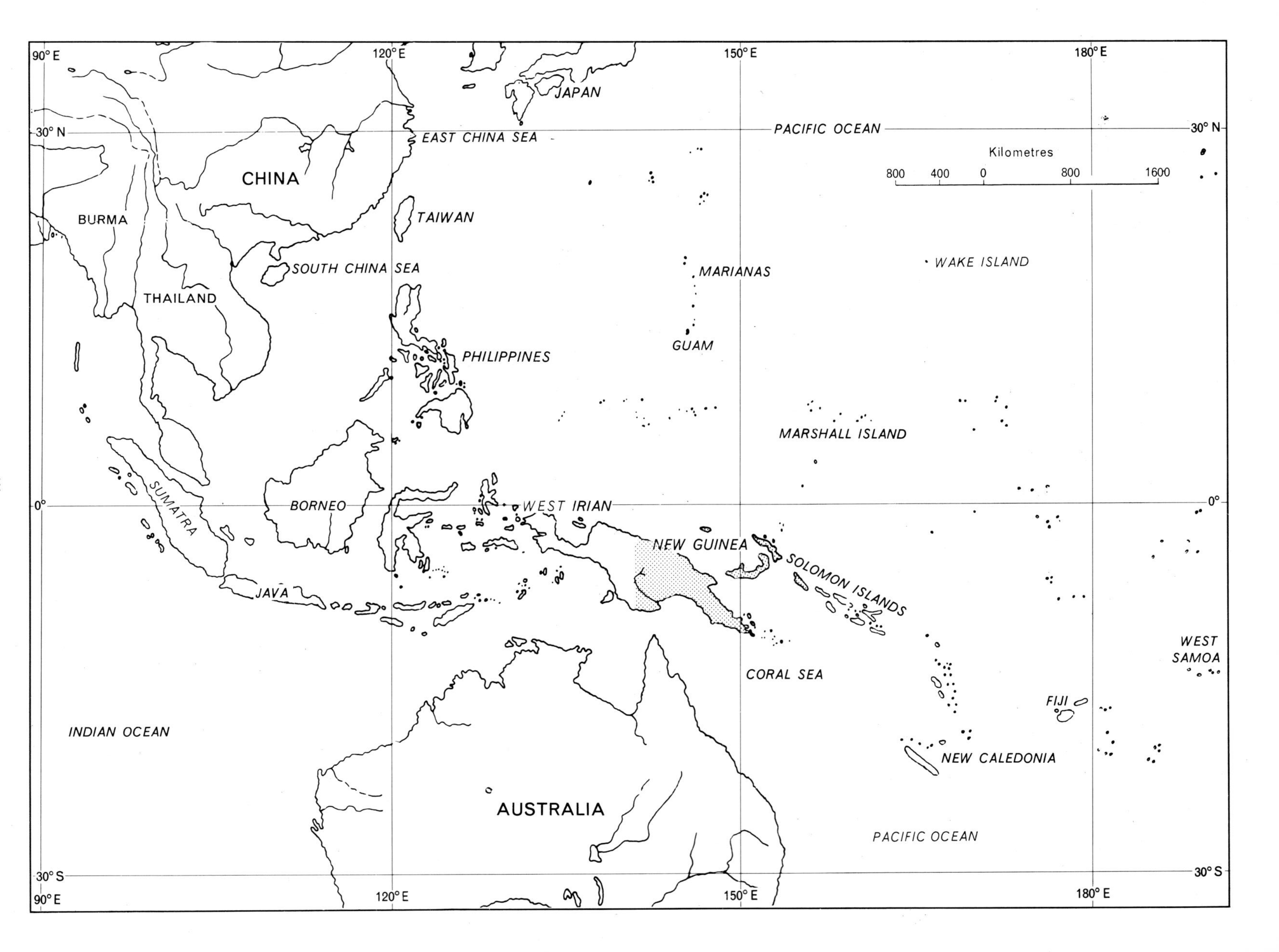

90° E
120° E
150° E
180° E
30° N
0°
30° S
JAPAN
PACIFIC OCEAN
EAST CHINA SEA
Kilometres
800
400
0
800
1600
CHINA
BURMA
TAIWAN
SOUTH CHINA SEA
MARIANAS
WAKE ISLAND
THAILAND
GUAM
PHILIPPINES
MARSHALL ISLAND
SUMATRA
BORNEO
WEST IRIAN
NEW GUINEA
SOLOMON ISLANDS
JAVA
WEST SAMOA
CORAL SEA
FIJI
INDIAN OCEAN
NEW CALEDONIA
AUSTRALIA
PACIFIC OCEAN

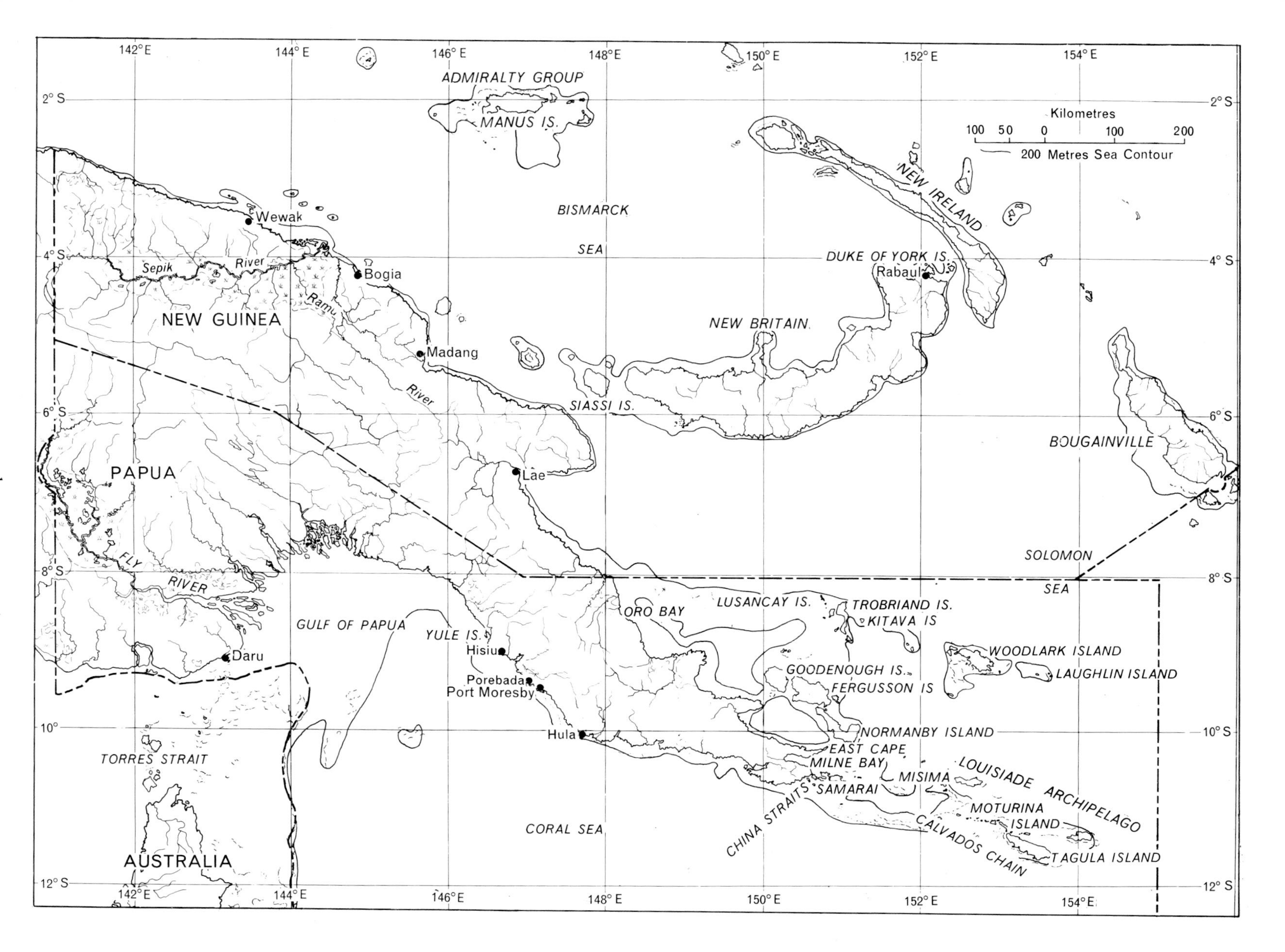
142° E
144° E
146° E
148° E
150° E
152° E
154° E
2° S
4° S
6° S
8° S
10°
10° S
12° S
ADMIRALTY GROUP
MANUS IS.
Kilometres
100 50 0 100 200
200 Metres Sea Contour
NEW IRELAND
BISMARCK
SEA
Wewak
Sepik
River
Bogia
Ramu
NEW GUINEA
Madang
River
DUKE OF YORK IS.
Rabaul
NEW BRITAIN
SIASSI IS.
BOUGAINVILLE
PAPUA
Lae
SOLOMON
SEA
FLY
RIVER
ORO BAY
LUSANCAY IS.
TROBRIAND IS.
KITAVA IS
GULF OF PAPUA
YULE IS.
Hisiu
Daru
WOODLARK ISLAND
LAUGHLIN ISLAND
GOODENOUGH IS.
FERGUSSON IS
Porebada
Port Moresby
Hula
NORMANBY ISLAND
EAST CAPE
MILNE BAY
MISIMA
LOUISIADE ARCHIPELAGO
SAMARAI
TORRES STRAIT
MOTURINA
ISLAND
CHINA STRAITS
CALVADOS CHAIN
CORAL SEA
TAGULA ISLAND
AUSTRALIA

FAMILY TROCHIDAE. Trochus and top shells.
There are several hundred species in this family inhabiting the world's seas. They range in size from the well-known commercial trochus which grows to 130 mm and larger to minute, sometimes delicately sculptured forms of 2·5 mm. Most are conical, with a high spire, but a few superficially resemble the turbans. Here is an example of the importance of retaining the opercula with live collected shells. All members of the Trochidae possess a round horny operculum, often paper thin. The Turbinidae have a solid shelly operculum.

1. **Trochus niloticus** LINNE. The commercial trochus, which, until replaced by synthetics, was harvested for its hard lustrous shell so much in demand for the manufacture of buttons and trinkets. Average width 100 mm.
2. **Trochus pyramis** BORN. A large species with a flat base and high tapering spire; ornamented in brown and green; base white. Common. Average width 60 mm.
3. **Trochus maculatus** LINNE. Port Moresby. Indo-Pacific range. A common species, attractively ornamented in variable shades of red and white; spiral rows of beads decorate the sides and base. Average width 40 mm.
4. **Trochus incrassatus** LAMARCK. Port Moresby. Reasonably common. Not as tall as preceding species which it resembles. Surface densely beaded; coloured greenish-white, with axial wavy streaks of reddish-brown. Average width 30 mm.
5. **Trochus fenestratus** GMELIN. Yule Island, Papua. Indo-Pacific range. Common. A steeply conical shell with a row of large knobs on each whorl. Off-white, marked with green between knobs; base flat and white. Average width 25 mm.
6. **Trochus tubiferus** KIENER. Port Moresby. Indo-Pacific range. Moderately common. A small shell with a row of spinous knobs on each whorl; a greyish colour, marked irregularly with brown, green and white; base heavily ornamented with wavy radial brown lines. Average width 25 mm.
7. **Trochus laciniatus** REEVE. Yule Island, Papua. Uncommon. A small shell; surface heavily beaded and with one row of slightly larger beads on each whorl; greenish-grey, ornamented with wide wavy axial bands of reddish-brown; base off-white, densely beaded and flecked with red. Averages 20 mm.
8. **Astele bularra** GARRARD. From 65 fathoms, south Queensland. Scarce. Of light texture, this shell is delicately sculptured with spaced rows of raised beads; coloured fawn to yellow, with a row of brown dashes above suture. To 25 mm.
9. **Euchelus atratus** GMELIN. Yule Island, Papua. Indo-Pacific range. A small common species; whorls rounded; aperture wide and nacreous; dark grey to olive green; spiral rows of coarse beads and white spots. Average width 20 mm.
10. **Chrysostoma paradoxum** BORN. A common shell on intertidal reefs; very active at night. Indo-Pacific range. Smooth; whorls rounded; attractively and variably coloured in shades of brown and red; columella red; inside aperture is iridescent gold. Averages 15 mm.

FAMILY TURBINIDAE. The turbans have inflated and rounded body whorls, and the aperture is covered internally by a pearly layer. The opercula are solid, calcareous, and fill the aperture. (The largest member of the family, the Green Snail, *Turbo marmoratus*, is collected commercially.)

11. **Turbo petholatus** LINNE. Madang, New Guinea. Indo-Pacific range. A common species that prefers the outer seaward fringe of reefs and rocky shorelines. Smooth; beautifully ornamented in brown and green in an extremely variable pattern. The operculum, the "cat's eye", is as well known as the shell. Average length 45 mm.
12. **Turbo chrysostoma** LINNE. Samarai, Papua. Indo-Pacific distribution. Common. Surface rough due to several ridges and two rows of spines. Coloured cream to pale green with axial bands and blotches of brown; aperture yellow-gold deepening to bright orange within. Average length 45 mm.
13. **Turbo argyrostoma** LINNE. Port Moresby. Indo-Pacific range. Common. A cream shell with patches of green and brown, and broken lines of black; aperture white. Averages 45 mm.
14. **Turbo porphyrites** GMELIN. Yule Island, Papua. Indo-Pacific range. Spire low and rounded; numerous fine axial ribs; cream, flecked with red and brown. Average length 40 mm.
15. **Turbo necnivosus** IREDALE. Port Moresby. Indo-Pacific distribution. Common. Numerous low beaded spiral ribs; cream to yellow, variably ornamented with blotches and spots of reddish-brown; aperture white, tinted yellow on inner columella surface. Average length 25 mm.
16. **Astralium calcar** LINNE. Samarai, Papua. Indo-Pacific distribution. Uncommon. A quaintly formed little shell, appearing deformed by the angle of the whorls, and the protruding fins on the outer periphery. White to yellow; base with a tint of mauve. Average length 20 mm.

FAMILY ANGARIIDAE. A small family of shells, of medium sizes, with depressed spire, rough or spinose surface, and a round aperture with a horny operculum similar to that of the Trochidae.

17. **Angaria delphina** LINNE. Port Moresby. Indo-Pacific distribution. Common. Shell is covered with spiral rows of spines, the row at shoulder usually much produced. Aperture large, round and nacreous. Averages 50 mm.

FAMILY LITTORINIDAE. Most of the members of this family live on rocks, mangroves and wharf piles in the intertidal zone, and many live above high water level.

18. **Tectarius pagodus** LINNE. Trobriand Islands, Papua. Indo-Pacific distribution. Lives in colonies in rock crevices well above high tide mark. Shell is cream to grey; curved axial folds; and two rows of spines; aperture round, cream within, with reddish-brown lirae; operculum thin and horny. Average length 45 mm.

FAMILY XENOPHORIDAE. The carrier shells attach stones, sand, and other shells and shell fragments to their own shells. The shells are conical, with a flat base. The operculum is paper thin and horny.

19 & 20. Xenophora torrida KURODA. Rabaul, New Britain. Central Indo-Pacific range. Uncommon. A dark brown shell; base with raised radial ridges; umbilicus closed. Of several specimens examined from Rabaul area, all were decorated with sand and small stones, none with shell attachments. Average width 40 mm.

21 & 22. Xenophora corrugata REEVE. Dredged 74 metres, Queensland. Occurs from China Sea to Australia, in deep water. Not common. A whitish shell; base white, lined with reddish-brown; umbilicus closed. Stones, sand and shells indiscriminately attached. Averages 40 mm.

23 & 24. Onustus exutus REEVE. 37 metres, Gulf of Papua. Distribution, China Sea to New Guinea. Reasonably common. A thin, conical, fawn-coloured shell, with little or no debris attachments. Some specimens have fine sand only cemented near apex. The base of the body whorl is produced into a broad thin appendage, scalloped at the periphery. Base cream and smooth, with fine radial ribs; umbilicus widely open. Average width 45 mm.

25 & 26. Xenophora solarioides REEVE. Dredged off Yule Island, Papua. Uncommon. A small white shell, densely encrusted with shells and shell fragments. Some specimens with small pebbles near apex, but shells are predominant. Base white; umbilicus open. Averages 20 mm.

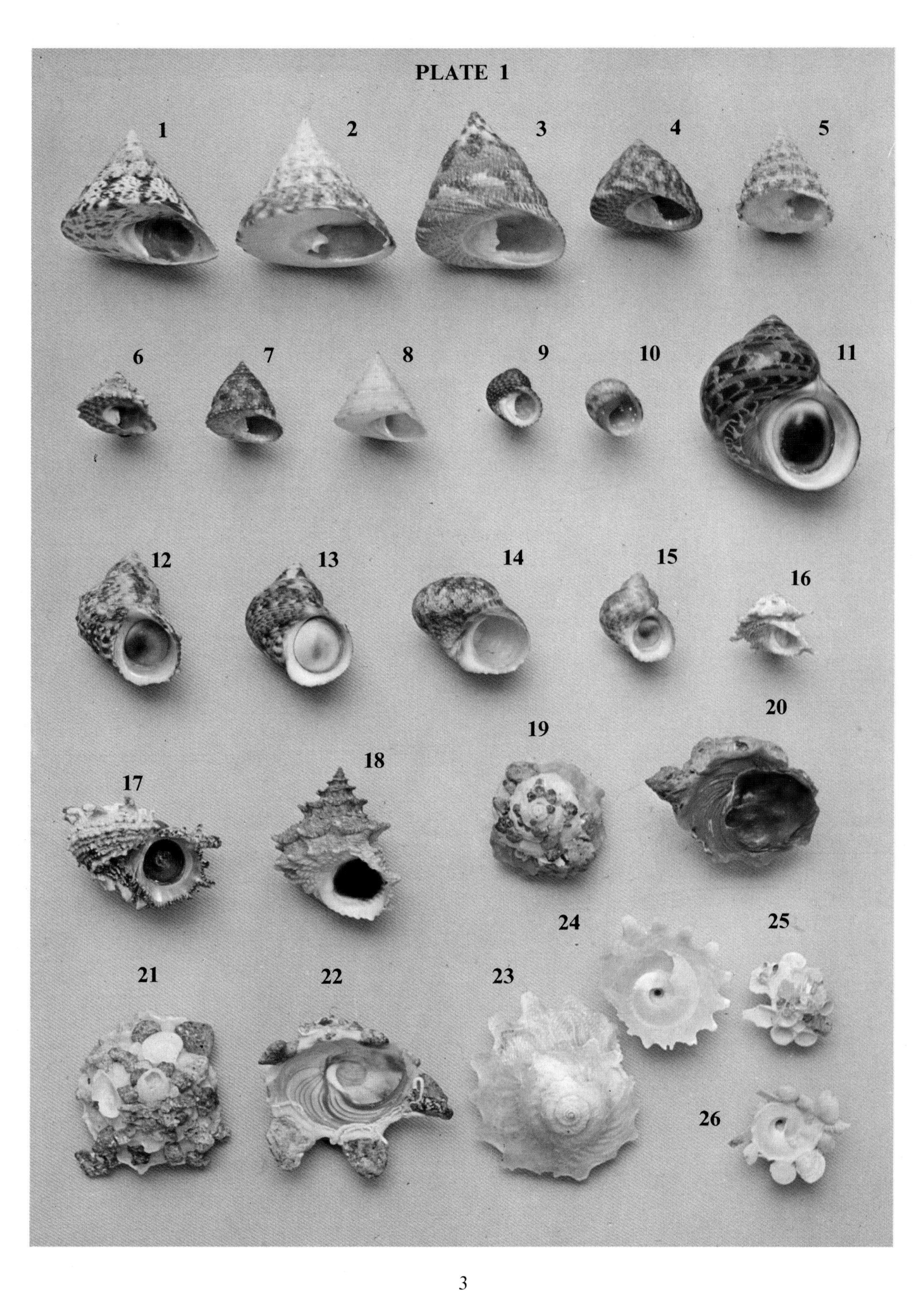
PLATE 1
1
2
3
4
5
6
7
8
9
10
11
12
13
14
15
16
17
18
19
20
21
22
23
24
25
26

FAMILY POTAMIDIDAE. The mud whelks are usually found in large colonies on intertidal mud and mangrove flats, and are related to the Cerithiidae. The operculum is circular, horny, with nucleus at centre.

1. **Pyrazus ebeninus** BRUG. A solid shell, found in large numbers on river and bay mud flats along the northern coastline of Australia. Average length 75 mm.

2. **Telescopium telescopium** LINNE. A common species on intertidal mangrove-fringed shorelines. North Australia and New Guinea. Average length 75 mm.

3. **Terebralia sulcata** BORN. Port Moresby Harbour. Distribution Indo-Pacific. Common. Average length on Papuan coast is 30 mm, but grows to 65 mm in north Australia.

FAMILY CERITHIIDAE. In visible shell characters, the creepers are hard to separate from their close relatives, the mud whelks; the main difference being in the shape and formation of the operculum. Cerithiidae have a horny operculum, sub-circular in shape, and the nucleus is off centre. The creepers inhabit the open reefs, lagoons and sand flats, from the tide-line to several metres depth.

4 to 6. Cerithium species. Intertidal sand and mud flats, Port Moresby Harbour. Very common shells that, despite the remarkable variation in sculpture and colour, are obviously closely related. Further research desirable before species can be satisfactorily separated.

7. **Cerithium echinatum** LAMARCK. Dredged 15 metres Port Moresby Harbour. A fawn shell with dark apex; fine axial grooves; longitudinal ridges, raised and nodulose at shoulder of whorl. Average length 30 mm.

8. **Cerithium asperum** LINNE. Port Moresby. Indo-Pacific distribution. Common. Usually all-white; sculpture consisting of spiral and axial ridges about evenly spaced, giving a latticed appearance. Average length 50 mm.

9. **Ochetoclava articulata** A. ADAMS & REEVE. On sand, 4 metres, Yule Island, Papua. A white shell, blotched and flecked with brown. Numerous spiral rows of fine beads. Average length 45 mm.

10. **Cerithium vertagus** LINNE. Port Moresby. Common species from shallow water throughout the Indo-Pacific. A smooth, white shell with light brown band and rib-like longitudinal folds below sutures. Odd specimens are all white. Averages 55 mm.

11. **Cerithium vertagus** LINNE. An odd form from 5·5 metres off Yule Island, Papua. A large, white shell, with two rows of light brown axial bars; rib-like folds below sutures. 80 mm.

12. **Cerithium nodulosum** BRUG. Yule Island, Papua. Indo-Pacific distribution. Common on shallow sand close to coral reefs. A large, heavy shell; cream in colour, irregularly marked with dark brown; a row of prominent nodules on whorls. Average length 75 mm.

13. **Cerithium aluco** LINNE. Port Moresby. Indo-Pacific distribution. Common. A solid shell; cream, with spots and fleckings of reddish-brown; a row of spaced nodules high on each whorl. Average length 65 mm.

14. **Cerithium sinensis** GMELIN. Port Moresby. Indo-Pacific distribution. Common. A stout shell, attractively decorated with rows of granulated ridges etched in alternating brown and white spots, and with odd large patches of brown; a row of spinous nodules below suture. Average length 60 mm.

15 to 17. Cerithium fasciatum BRUG. Yule Island, Papua. Indo-Pacific distribution. Common. A solid, smooth and shining shell; white, with spiral bands of variable width in light to dark brown. Odd specimens are all white. Longitudinal folding ridges most prominent below sutures. Surprisingly variable colour patterns even in the one population. Averages 65 mm.

FAMILY JANTHINIDAE. The violet snails are mostly found on ocean beaches after strong winds. They manufacture an air float, and spend their life drifting on the surface of the sea.

18. **Janthina janthina** LINNE. Trobriand Islands, eastern Papua. Abundant throughout the Indo-Pacific. Average width 25 mm.

FAMILY SILIQUARIIDAE. The tube or worm shells are grotesquely twisted and coiled. They have a narrow slit which often runs the full length of the coiled shell. Usually attached to sponges, coral, or underside of boulders.

19. **Siliquaria cumingi** MÖRCH. Rabaul, New Britain. Smooth; cream to light brown; a row of holes becomes a continuous slit towards aperture.

20. **Siliquaria muricata** BORN. Lusancay Islands, eastern Papua. A mauve coloured shell, with a black lined slit running full length of coils. Coils are spinous on undersides.

FAMILY TURRITELLIDAE. Members of this family are long and regularly coiled like the terebras or augers, but their whorls are more rounded and are coarsely and spirally sculptured with a dull finish. The aperture is simple, rather small and almost circular, lacking any plications or thickening of the outer lip.

21. **Haustator cingulifera** REEVE. Dredged from 15 metres off the Sepik River, New Guinea. A small Indo-Pacific species averaging 20 mm in length. Cream to light brown, with darker band at sutures; raised spiral ridges; whorls slightly flattened.

22. **Turritella terebra** LINNE. Dredged from 30 metres, Gulf of Papua, where it is abundant. Indo-Pacific distribution. A large comparatively smooth species; whorls rounded; fawn to brown in colour; fine spiral grooves and curved growth lines. Average length 100 mm.

FAMILY ARCHITECTONICIDAE. These attractive shells are commonly referred to as the sundials. They are flat based, lowly conical, and circular. Their umbilicus is widely open, circular, and sculptured with spiral ridges like a winding staircase.

23. **Architectonica perspectiva** LINNE. An unusual colour form from the Admiralty Islands. See also 26 and 27 below.

24 and 25. Architectonica maxima PHILIPPI. Dredged from 45 metres off Queensland coast. A large attractive species. Has deep spiral grooves crossed by axial ridges, giving a beaded appearance. Blue-grey on early whorls, fawn below. Spiral rows of squarish brown spots on dorsum and base. Average width 50 mm.

26 and 27. Architectonica perspectiva LINNE. Dredged from 9 metres off the Sepik River, New Guinea. Indo-Pacific distribution. Smoother than preceding species, with fine slightly-curved axial grooves. Fawn in colour, spirally banded with white and dark brown. Average width 40 mm.

28. **Heliacus variegatus** GMELIN. Intertidal, Port Moresby. Indo-Pacific distribution. A common, shallow water species that is sometimes classified under a separate family, Heliacidae. Base of shell rounded. Entire surface is coarsely corded and spirally banded with alternating dark brown and white squarish spots. Average width 15 mm.

29. **Philippia radiata** RÖDING. Rabaul, New Britain. Indo-Pacific distribution. A smooth, polished shell with two spiral grooves on lower part of body whorl. White, with a broad brown band below suture. In some specimens the brown "runs" from lower edge of colour band towards the periphery, in axial streaks. Average width 20 mm.

PLATE 2
1
2
4
3
5
6
7
8
9
10
11
12
13
14
15
16
17
18
19
20
22
23
21
28
24
25
26
27
29

FAMILY STROMBIDAE. The tibias, strombs, conches and spider shells. Strombs are herbivorous feeders, and are most prolific in the shallow waters of the tropical Indo-Pacific. The shells are mostly solid, with a thickened flaring lip. A characteristic feature is a well developed notch in the lip at the anterior end. The group contains some of the largest, most colourful, and ornamental forms of marine gastropods, and all but a few are available to the average collector. Members of this family have an unusual and ungainly method of locomotion. The strong muscular foot propels the animal, both forward and backwards, in a series of hopping movements. When placed on its back, the animal can extend its foot and right itself with one thrust. In adult specimens the operculum is long, sharp and slightly curved.

1. **Tibia fusus** LINNE. From Taiwan to South-east Asia, at depths to 40 metres. A scarce shell, it is a showpiece in a display cabinet. Average length 230 mm.
2. **Tibia powisi** PETIT. Figured specimen from 40 metres, Gulf of Papua. Occurs from Taiwan to north Australia in deep water. Uncommon. Average length 65 mm.
3. **Tibia insulae-chorab** RÖDING. Distribution — northern shores of the Indian Ocean to South-east Asia. This species only rarely occurs along the western limits of the central Indo-Pacific, but is illustrated and included here because of the popularity of this genus with shell collectors. An uncommon shell, heavier than preceding species, averaging 140 mm in length.
4. **Strombus lentiginosus** LINNE. Port Moresby. A common attractive species throughout the tropical Indo-Pacific. Occurs on intertidal sand flats near coral reefs. Average length 75 mm.
5. **Strombus lentiginosus** LINNE. Juvenile form lacking the thickened and flaring lip of adult specimens.
6. **Strombus pipus** RÖDING. Siassi Islands, western New Britain. Distribution — Indo-Pacific, from low tide line to 10 metres, near coral reefs. Uncommon. Average length 65 mm.
7. **Strombus aurisdianae** LINNE. Yule Island, Papua. Distribution — Indian Ocean and western Pacific. A common and attractive species of intertidal zones and shallow sandy lagoons, close to coral reefs. To 80 mm.
8. **Strombus aratrum** RÖDING. Port Moresby. Distribution — north-eastern Australia and south Papuan coast. Occurs on intertidal sand and mud flats near coral reefs. Apart from the dark coloration of the upper columellar surface and outer lip, this species is narrower in the body whorl, and with a more produced spire than *S. aurisdianae*. From 65 mm to 90 mm.
9. **Strombus bulla** RÖDING. Manus Island, Admiralty Group. Distribution — central Indo-Pacific. Not as widely distributed as *S. aurisdianae* which it closely resembles. *S. bulla* has a slightly wider aperture and smoother dorsal surface. The tip of the spire and the edges of the siphonal canal are tinted lavender. Averages 50 mm.
10. **Strombus bulla** RÖDING. Ventral view.
11. **Strombus vomer** RÖDING. North-west Australia. Distribution — occurs in small isolated populations in the western Pacific where it is fairly common. A slightly larger shell than the previous species, with aperture wider, stained yellow, and containing numerous white lirae. Average length 90 mm.
12. **Strombus luhuanus** LINNE. Port Moresby. A very common shell, inhabiting the intertidal flats to about 10 metres, from Indonesia and New Guinea to Fiji. A heavy shell averaging 50 mm in length, that is easily recognized by the chocolate-brown columella and red outer lip.
13. **Strombus epidromis** LINNE. Samarai, eastern Papua. Distribution — restricted to the central Indo-Pacific. Between 65 mm and 100 mm, and rather scarce. The white aperture and flaring, rounded lip make this species one of the most graceful of the strombs.
14. **Strombus epidromis** LINNE. Ventral view.
15. **Strombus vittatus** LINNE. Dredged 27 metres, Gulf of Papua. This rather thin-shelled, tall spired form which appears to have its centre of distribution in New Guinea waters, is a deepwater species. Scarce. A smooth shell, some specimens with a weak knob on dorsum.
16. **Strombus vittatus** LINNE. A heavier shell than preceding form, usually with a pronounced knob on dorsum. Occurs north and west Australia. Average length 55 mm.
17. **Strombus dilatatus** SWAINSON. Dredged from 15 metres off Yule Island, Gulf of Papua. An uncommon shell restricted to central Indo-Pacific, offshore on sand and mud bottom. A solid shell, flaring outer lip; columella and lip white; reddish-purple patch within aperture, crossed by white spiral lirae. Lip extends onto the third prewhorl of the spire. Average length 60 mm.
18. **Strombus canarium** LINNE. An unusually large form, with stepped spire, from Manus Island, Admiralty Group. Distribution — tropical and subtropical waters of the central Indo-Pacific. A common and extremely variable species over the range, and even in individual populations. Found on intertidal sand and mud flats. This form attains 90 mm.
19. **Strombus canarium** LINNE. Typical form, abundant along the Papuan coast. Average length 50 mm.
20. **Strombus canarium** LINNE. From Hula, Papuan coast, where it occurs with the more typical form above. Average length 65 mm.
21. **Strombus canarium** LINNE. The featured specimen collected at Porebada, Papuan coast, is semi-albinistic, with a faint golden reticulated pattern on the dorsum.
22. **Strombus canarium** LINNE. An albinistic form collected rarely among colonies of the typical form. Scarce on the Papuan coast, rare elsewhere. Average length 50 mm.

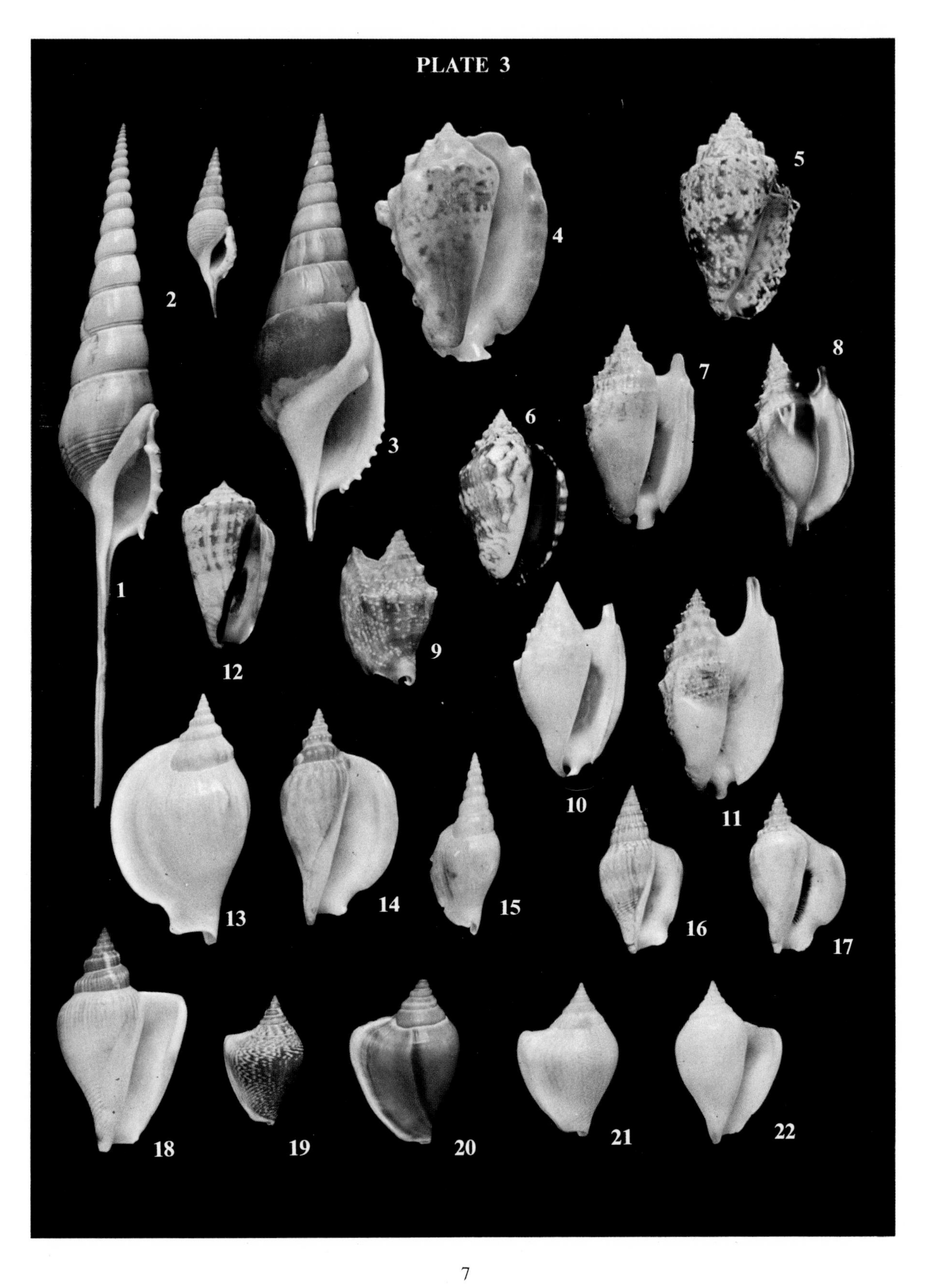
PLATE 3
1
2
3
4
5
6
7
8
9
10
11
12
13
14
15
16
17
18
19
20
21
22

FAMILY STROMBIDAE — continued.

1. **Strombus thersites** SWAINSON. A large, heavy stromb, much prized by collectors. Taken occasionally in prawn trawl nets, and by divers, from below the tide line to about 30 metres depth in the Ryukyu Islands, Taiwan, Eastern Papua, New Caledonia and possibly on the offshore reefs at the northern fringes of the Great Barrier Reef. Featured specimen from 15 metres, Moturina Island, off eastern Papua. An extremely heavy shell, usually between 130 mm and 170 mm in length.
2. **Strombus latissimus** LINNE. Distribution and habitat similar to preceding species, with records from Fiji. A large, heavy shell with unusually thickened edge to outer lip, often handsomely marked in brown and cream wavy axial pattern, and a glossy salmon-pink tint on the flaring lip. Not as rare as *S. thersites*, but not at all common. The figured specimen from Manus Island in the Admiralty Group, where native skin divers collect occasional specimens in 6 to 12 metres of water on sandy bottom in gutters between coral reefs. Attains 200 mm.
3. **Strombus sinuatus** HUMPHREY. Trobriand Islands. Distribution — central Indo-Pacific, on coral sand bottom adjacent to coral reefs from 4 to 18 metres. Appears more frequently on offshore islands, and is collected occasionally in small colonies, by native fishermen in the Louisiade Archipelago, eastern Papua. A really beautiful shell in both shape and colour. It is solid, but not as gross as preceding species, and has a recurved and very deep stromboid notch. Average length 115 mm.
4. **Lambis lambis** LINNE. A juvenile specimen of the common spider shell.
5. **Lambis lambis** LINNE. Semi-juvenile specimen.
6. **Lambis lambis** LINNE. Port Moresby. Distribution — tropical Indo-Pacific, in shallow water, on or near coral reefs. A common shell throughout its range. Average length 130 mm, but odd specimens grow to 200 mm.
7. **Lambis crocata** LINK. Samarai, eastern Papua. Distribution — tropical Indo-Pacific. Prefers sloping reefs, at 3 to 10 metres depth. This uncommon species is readily recognized by its narrow aperture which is of a uniform orange colour, and the anterior canal is long and curved. Average length 115 mm.
8. **Lambis scorpius** LINNE. Yule Island, Papua. Distribution — Indian Ocean and central Indo-Pacific. Prefers similar habit to previous species. Not common. Quite distinct in form and colour from related species, and easily recognized from the illustration. Averages 115 mm.
9. **Lambis millepeda** LINNE. Trobriand Islands. Distribution — restricted in the central Indo-Pacific to Philippines, Indonesia and New Guinea. Reasonably common within this range. Larger and heavier than preceding species, with more numerous, but shorter digitations. Adult specimens usually covered with coral growths and corroded. Young specimens make better display shells. Averages 130 mm.
10. **Lambis chiragra** LINNE. A juvenile form collected on north coast of New Britain. Large colonies of hermit crabs inhabiting these shells indicate a high mortality rate in these juveniles. The frail shell offers little protection, and the large fleshy animal must tempt many predators.
11. **Lambis chiragra** LINNE. A semi-juvenile form, which is very attractive at this stage of development.
12. **Lambis chiragra** LINNE. Figured specimen from Louisiade Archipelago, eastern Papua, where the shell is common. Distribution — tropical Indo-Pacific. Little variation over the range, though the male and female are distinct. The figured specimen is a typical female. The males are smaller with the columella heavily stained with purple-brown, with overlaying white spiral lirae. Average length 200 mm.
13. **Lambis truncata** HUMPHREY. Trobriand Islands. Distribution — Indo-Pacific. The largest and heaviest of the spider shells, averaging 280 mm in length. Aged specimens usually with columella and lip coloured mauve-brown, but semi-juvenile shells, such as the specimen illustrated, are creamy-white, and more attractive. They are reasonably common, and prefer the shallow water, 1 to 6 metres, with rubble coral and coarse sand bottom.

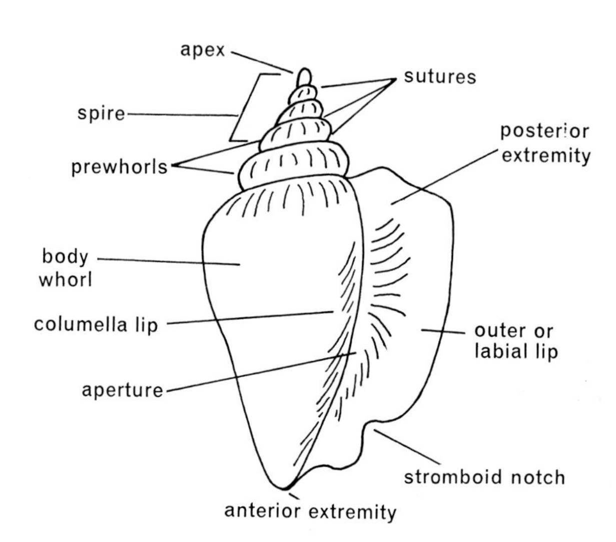

PLATE 4
1
2
3
4
5
6
7
8
9
10
11
12
13

FAMILY STROMBIDAE — continued.

1 and 2. Strombus gibberulus LINNE. Port Moresby. Distribution, Indo-Pacific. A very common shell on intertidal sand flats. Recognized by a distorted shape caused by a swelling of the penultimate whorl dorsally. Columella and inner lip edge lined with purple Averages 45 mm.

3. Strombus gibberulus LINNE. Samarai, eastern Papua. A colour variant with rose-tinted aperture.

4. Strombus variabilis SWAINSON. Porebada, Papua. Distribution — central Indo-Pacific. An uncommon species from low tide to about 25 metres. A variable species regarding coloration. Average length 45 mm.

5. Strombus variabilis SWAINSON. A variation with a large blotch on columella. Figured specimen from north Queensland.

6. Strombus variabilis SWAINSON. A pale form dredged from 22 metres, Gulf of Papua.

7 and 8. Strombus marginatus septimus DUCLOS. North coast of New Britain. Distribution — central Indo-Pacific. Not common. A smooth shell, dark brown, with five or six spiral rows of broken white lines. Average length 45 mm.

9 and 10. Strombus mutabilis SWAINSON. Samarai, eastern Papua. Distribution — Indo-Pacific. A common species, intertidal to a couple of metres depth. Variable in colour, but fairly consistent in other characters. Upper part of outer lip turns at a sharp angle giving the shells a distinct quadrate shape. Rose-pink inside aperture. Averages 30 mm.

11. Strombus mutabilis SWAINSON. A uniform orange coloured variety from Yule Island, Papua. Not common.

12. Strombus mutabilis SWAINSON. Port Moresby. A scarce colour variant.

13. Strombus erythrinus DILLWYN. Rabaul, New Britain. Distribution — found in various forms throughout the Indo-Pacific, but not at all common. Smoother than a similar species, *S. labiatus*. Another distinguishing feature is the regular, fine pattern on the body whorl, of fine spiral grooves and raised axial riblets, giving a granular appearance. From 20 to 40 mm.

14. Strombus urceus LINNE. Port Moresby. Distribution — central Indo-Pacific. Abundant on intertidal sand and mud flats. An extremely variable species. Most distinguishing features being the dark coloration on the outer surface of the long, slightly curved siphonal canal, and the narrow aperture that reaches the shoulder of the body whorl. Average length 40 mm.

15. Strombus urceus LINNE. Form with yellow aperture from Rabaul, New Britain.

16 to 18. Strombus labiatus RÖDING. Port Moresby. Distribution — central Indo-Pacific. Common. Similar to preceding species, but has wider and shorter aperture which does not reach to shoulder, and the siphonal canal is shorter and less recurved. Average length 40 mm.

19 and 20. Strombus microurceus KIRA. Dredged Port Moresby Harbour. Distribution — central Indo-Pacific. Relatively common. A small species resembling *S. labiatus*, but smoother, and aperture is wider and longer, nearly reaching the shoulder. 20 to 25 mm.

21. Strombus dentatus LINNE. Manus Island, Admiralty Group. Distribution — Indo-Pacific. An uncommon and attractive species from shallow water to 30 metres and more. A distinctive shell easily identified from illustration. Average length 40 mm.

22. Strombus fragilis RÖDING. Samarai, eastern Papua. Distribution — south-west Pacific. Uncommon. Similar in general appearance to previous species, but is lighter in weight, smoother, and lacks the spines on anterior end of aperture which is a typical characteristic of *S. dentatus*. Average length 40 mm.

23. Strombus plicatus pulchellus REEVE. Dredged 22 metres Port Moresby Harbour. Distribution — central Indo-Pacific. A fairly scarce shell in good condition. This attractive species can be identified by the deep brown colour inside the aperture, crossed by spiral lirae extending to the outer lip. Average length 30 mm.

24. Strombus labiosus WOOD. Dredged Bougainville Island, 22 metres. Distribution — Indian Ocean and western Pacific. Seldom found in good condition, but dead specimens appear common in dredgings throughout New Guinea. A small solid shell; aperture white; lip wide and flaring, sharply angled at upper extremity. Average length 25 mm.

25 and 26. Strombus minimus LINNE. North coast of New Britain, where it is common on weed-covered bottom from 1 to 4 metres depth. Distribution — Indonesia and New Guinea to Fiji. A solid, attractive little shell with its yellow aperture, brown coloured dorsum, and flaring lip extending upwards to the third suture. Average length 30 mm.

27 to 30. Terebellum terebellum LINNE. Port Moresby. Distribution — Indo-Pacific. Common. Lives in sand patches close to coral reefs, intertidal to several metres depth. A smooth, bullet-shaped shell; white or cream variably marked with blotches, spots and thin lines. Averages 50 mm.

31 and 32. Rimella cancellata LINNE. Dredged New Britain, where this shell is reasonably common. Appears scarce elsewhere. Distribution — central Indo-Pacific. Dorsum is fawn, with three spiral bands of light brown. The posterior canal extends almost to the apex of the spire, in a curving line. Close-set axial ribs are crossed by punctate spiral grooves, giving a fine granulated pattern. Average length 30 mm.

FAMILY EPITONIIDAE. The wentletraps are numerous, and range in size down to minute species that are parasitic on anemones and soft sponges. Two of the larger forms that have long been popular with collectors because of their exquisite shape and sculpture, are featured here.

33. Epitonium scalare LINNE. A quaint shell, delicately sculptured, and usually white to cream. Once a great rarity, now taken in reasonable numbers in dredgings and prawn trawl nets. Figured specimen from 40 metres off Yule Island, Gulf of Papua. Distribution — Japan to Australia. Average length 45 mm.

34. Epitonium pallasi KIENER. Dredged north Queensland. Distribution — Japan to Queensland. Uncommon. Smaller than preceding species; body whorl brown; fin-like varices white. Average length 25 mm.

PLATE 5
1
2
3
4
5
6
7
8
9
10
11
12
13
14
15
16
17
18
19
20
21
22
23
24
25
26
27
28
29
30
31
32
33
34

FAMILY CYMATIIDAE. A popular family of shells, the best known member being the beautiful Pacific trumpet, *Charonia tritonis*, illustrated on Plate 7. Form and sculpture is extremely variable in this family, making a general description difficult. A few are comparatively smooth and polished; some have deep spiral and axial grooves; whilst others are coarsely sculptured with elevated nodules and beaded cords. All cymatids have a well developed multispiral operculum that usually completely seals the aperture.

1. **Distorsio anus** LINNE. Port Moresby. Distribution — Indo-Pacific. Common. A heavy shell; white with spiral bands of brown; latter whorls distorted; aperture constricted and strongly toothed. Average length 55 mm.
2. **Distorsio reticulata** RÖDING. Dredged 27 metres, Gulf of Papua. Indo-Pacific range. Uncommon. Narrower than preceding species; aperture mauve to reddish-brown with strong white teeth. Figured specimen with periostracum. Average length 50 mm.
3. **Cymatium nicobaricum** RÖDING. Samarai, Eastern Papua. Distribution — Indo-Pacific. Uncommon. A solid shell; white, with broad brown bands and fine spiral ribs and axial ridges; aperture orange with white teeth. To 65 mm.
4. **Cymatium pileare** LINNE. Intertidal, Port Moresby. Indo-Pacific range. Common. Cream to grey, heavily marked with dark brown; fine spiral and axial ridges; aperture red with strong white teeth. Average length 75 mm.
5. **Cymatium lotorium** LINNE. Samarai, eastern Papua. Indo-Pacific distribution. Uncommon. A thick, solid shell; large nodules at shoulder; fawn to orange; varices banded white and brown; aperture white. Averages 100 mm.
6. **Cymatium pyrum** LINNE. Port Moresby. Distribution — Indo-Pacific. Uncommon. Another heavy shell; one to four rows of nodules at shoulder; orange-brown; aperature similarly coloured, but white within; strong white teeth. To 100 mm.
7. **Cymatium sinensis** REEVE. A deepwater species from mid-Queensland coast. Uncommon. White to yellow; spaced spiral ribs, slightly nodulose; aperture white. To 65 mm.
8. **Cymatium gutturnium** RÖDING. Port Moresby. Indo-Pacific range. Uncommon. An extremely variable shell regarding colour. Figured specimen is white with axial streaks of brown; inside of aperture deep yellow. Some specimens have an orange aperture. Anterior canal is long and slightly curved. Average length 55 mm.
9. **Cymatium caudatum** GMELIN. Dredged 40 metres, Gulf of Papua. Indo-Pacific range. A scarce offshore species. Thin shell; all white in colour; rounded spaced ribs; deeply channelled suture; long anterior canal only slightly curved. Average length 55 mm.
10. **Cymatium hepaticum** RÖDING. Samarai, eastern Papua. Distribution — western Pacific. Uncommon. A solid, attractive shell; honey brown, with narrow spiral bands of dark brown; white lines on varices; aperture white; surface beaded. Average length 45 mm.
11. **Cymatium pfeifferianum** REEVE. 22 metres, Gulf of Papua. Indo-Pacific range. Uncommon. An attractive species; each whorl roundly inflated and beaded; fawn in colour, with two pairs of spiral brown lines separated by a broader cream band. Average length 65 mm.

12 to 14. Cymatium muricinum RÖDING. Port Moresby. Common throughout Indo-Pacific. A growth series illustrated. A solid, nodulose shell; white, with broad brown bands; adults with reddish-brown aperture and white callosity extending over parental wall. Average length 40 mm.

15. **Septa parthenopeum** VON SALIS. Yule Island, Papua. Distribution — Indo-Pacific. Reasonably common. A fawn shell, with brown and white bars on varices; aperture white; columella dark brown, with raised white lirae. Average length 75 mm.
16. **Septa gemmata** REEVE. Bougainville Island. Indo-Pacific range. Common. A small shell; white to yellow; decorated with beaded spiral ribs. Average length 30 mm.
17. **Septa rubecula** LINNE. Samarai, eastern Papua. Distribution — western Pacific. Uncommon. A small, solid shell; ornamented with spiral rows of beads; coloured orange to red, with one or two white bars on varices; aperture white; columella orange. Average length 30 mm.
18. **Gyrineum bituberculatis** LAMARCK. 22 metres, Port Moresby Harbour. Uncommon. Two opposing varices per whorl; shell slightly depressed; cream to fawn, with brown nodules in spiral rows; aperture white. Average length 40 mm.

FAMILY BURSIDAE. Commonly referred to as frog shells, the members of this family are very coarsely sculptured, and all have a well developed posterior canal. In most species, the old varices form two continuous ridges from the apex to the base, giving a flattened or depressed appearance.

19. **Bursa crumena** LAMARCK. 35 metres, Gulf of Papua. Indo-Pacific distribution. Common. Has three rows of sharp nodules per whorl, becoming small spines on varices; intermediate spiral rows of fine lines and beads; aperture and columella white. Average length 50 mm.
20. **Bursa rana** LINNE. 35 metres, Gulf of Papua. Indo-Pacific range. Common offshore. Narrower than preceding species, with more prominent spines. A white shell with light brown tonings. Average length 50 mm.
21. **Bursa margaritula** DESHAYES. 35 metres, Gulf of Papua. Not common. Small, light brown shell; heavily sculptured with spiral rows of beads, and one row of fin-like nodules, not spinous; aperture white; anterior canal pale lilac. Average length 25 mm.
22. **Bursa granularis** RÖDING. A common shell on intertidal reefs, along entire New Guinea coastline. Distribution — world wide. Light brown in colour; aperture cream to fawn; granulose surface. Average length 40 mm.
23. **Bursa rubeta** LINNE. Juvenile specimen, see Plate 7 No. 2.
24. **Bursa species.** Though not at all rare, this shell is apparently unnamed. Figured specimen collected in 6 metres of water on coral reef off Yule Island, Papua, where it is reasonably common. A heavy shell; two prominent knobs between opposing varices; old posterior canals open; white in colour, with blotches of purplish-brown; aperture purple with raised orange teeth. Average length 65 mm.
25. **Bursa bufonia** GMELIN. Dredged 18 metres, Yule Island, Papua. Uncommon. A heavy chunky shell; white, with spiral lines of brown; heavily noduled; aperture white. To 50 mm.
26. **Bursa rosa** PERRY. Samarai, eastern Papua. Indo-Pacific distribution. Uncommon. Solid; three low nodules between varices; yellow, with odd brown patches and spots; aperture purplish-brown. Average length 50 mm.
27. **Bursa cruentata** SOWERBY. Siassi Islands, western New Britain. Distribution — Indo-Pacific. Scarce shell. Small; white, with odd brown spots; decorated with a row of paired knobs on body whorl; aperture white, with five or six distinct purplish-brown dashes on columella. Average length 30 mm.

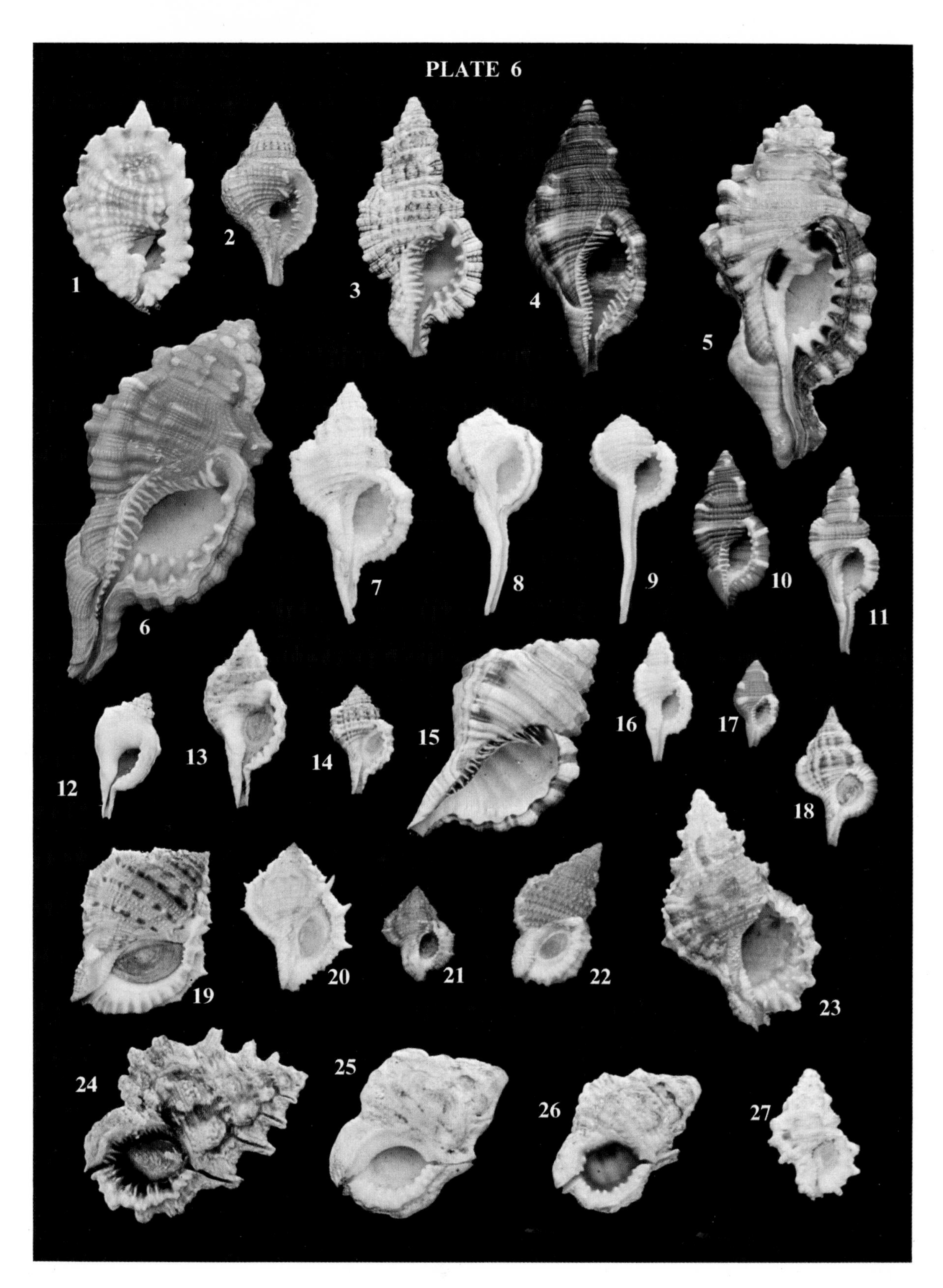
PLATE 6
1
2
3
4
5
6
7
8
9
10
11
12
13
14
15
16
17
18
19
20
21
22
23
24
25
26
27

This Plate illustrates some of the larger species of marine gastropods.

FAMILY CYMATIIDAE — Introduced on Plate 6.

1. **Charonia tritonis** LINNE. The Pacific trumpet shell. Figured specimen from Bougainville Island, where it is reasonably abundant on shallow coral reefs. Distribution, tropical Indo-Pacific. This shell is undoubtedly the most decorative of the larger ornamental shells. Apart from its beauty as a display specimen or general ornament, island people do actually use this shell as a trumpet. By drilling a hole in the tapering spire, about 75 mm from the apex, a deep vibrant note that carries for miles across the sea is produced. One of the known predators of the destructive Crown of Thorns Starfish, *Acanthaster planci*, the triton shell is now protected in north Australia. Average length 250 mm, but giants to at least 450 mm have been recorded.

FAMILY BURSIDAE — Introduced on Plate 6.

2. **Bursa rubeta** LINNE. Yule Island, Papua. Range — central Indo-Pacific. Uncommon. Prefers the outer seaward slope of heavy coral reefs. A rugged shell, usually heavily encrusted with coral growth. Aperture large and flaring; columella and outer lip deep yellow to orange; crossed on columella side with fine raised white plicae; inside lip with ten to twelve coarse raised plicae. Average length 180 mm.

3. **Bursa bubo** LINNE. Samarai, eastern Papua. Range — Indo-Pacific. Reasonably common. A heavy shell, similar in form to previous species, differing in having a paler aperture which is usually white to cream-yellow, and with columella plicae less produced. In this species the operculum has an extension or lip that fits over the posterior canal. This feature is lacking in *B. rubeta*. A large shell averaging 230 mm in length.

FAMILY CASSIDAE — Introduction on Plate 8.

4. **Cassis cornuta** LINNE. Samarai, eastern Papua. Indo-Pacific distribution. Common. The largest of the cassids, and a most decorative shell, with a heavy and colourful callosity about the aperture. One of the true "heavies" of the mollusc phylum. The shell is usually found partly buried in sand and broken coral rubble, and emerges to feed on the rising tide. A shallow water species which prefers a sandy habitat, close to large coral reef areas. Adult specimens average 305 mm, but odd ones much larger.

5. **Cassis rufa** LINNE. Trobriand Islands, eastern Papua. Distributed throughout the entire tropical Indo-Pacific and most abundant along the east African coast. The Italian cameo workers have used this shell in their craft for hundreds of years. Prefers shallow sand bottom close to coral reefs. A brilliant and attractive shell, and readily available to collectors. Best display specimens are those between 100 and 125 mm, when fully adult, but lacking heavy encrustation and damage to the dorsal surface. Average length 125 mm.

FAMILY TONNIDAE. Introduced on Plate 9.

6. **Tonna cerevisina** HEDLEY. From Queensland coast, where it is dredged in large numbers by prawn trawlers. Alternately banded with brown and white, with reddish-brown spots on white areas. A large shell, averaging 230 mm in length.

FAMILY GALEODIDAE (MELONGENIDAE). Members of this family are closely related to the **FASCIOLARIIDAE** and **BUCCINIDAE.**

7. **Syrinx aruanus** LINNE. 30 metres, Gulf of Papua. Ranges from north Australia to New Guinea. Reasonably common off-shore. The largest living gastropod, specimens in excess of 610 mm not uncommon. Usually taken by prawn trawlers in depths to 40 metres. Fawn to yellow-orange in colour; covered with a thick, light brown periostracum. The shell is not heavy considering its size, and the lip is usually chipped when taken from the nets.

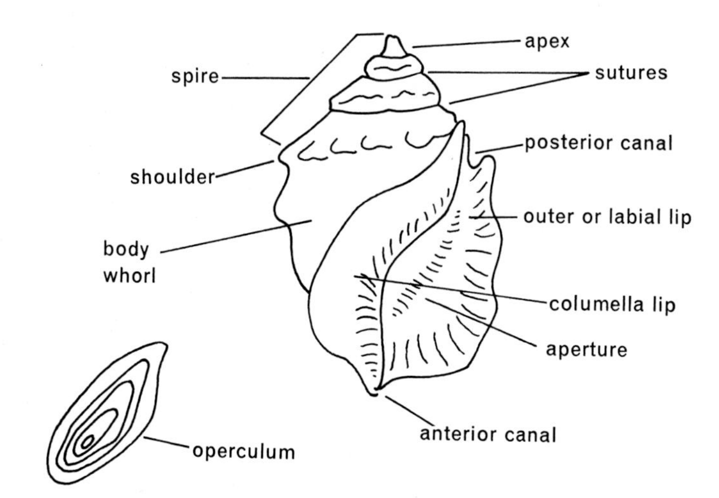

PLATE 7
1
2
3
4
7
6
5

FAMILY CASSIDAE. The helmet or bonnet shells are characterized by an ovate shape; large swollen body whorl and mostly a well-developed, and often colourful, outer lip and columella shield. Most but not all adult specimens have a fan-shaped operculum. There are less than two dozen living species in the tropical Indo-Pacific, ranging in size from 13 mm to the giant *Cassis cornuta* which attains 450 mm. However, the wide distributional range of some species, and their relative abundance, makes the family a well-known one, with many variations and forms, and some subspecies recognized. They are mostly shallow water dwellers, but odd specimens have been dredged from very deep water. The cassids are carnivores and some have been observed feeding on species of the long spined sea-urchins, diadema, and a few indicate a preference for this unlikely food. When inactive, during daylight hours, they bury in sand.

1 and 2. Phalium areola LINNE. Port Moresby. Distributed throughout the tropical Indo-Pacific, in shallow water. Has five rows of large square marks on body whorl, and former varices are strongly evident on spire. Specimens from shallow turbid waters are usually darker and with deeper spiral grooves than those from clear reef areas. A common species. Ranges from 40 to 75 mm in length.

3. Phalium bandatum PERRY. Trawled from 22 metres off Yule Island, Papua. Distribution — central Indo-Pacific, ranging from Japan to Australia. Intertidal to about 30 metres depth. A large, attractive and uncommon species; dorsum ornamented with five to six bands of light brown squarish marks, occasionally blending to become continuous bands. Attains 130 mm.

4. Phalium glaucum LINNE. Manus Island, Admiralty Group. Distribution — Indian Ocean and central Indo-Pacific. Dorsum blue-grey, with obsolete yellow-brown banding. A large shell often confused with previous species, but *P. glaucum* is more swollen ovate; has less produced spire; and has three or four prominent spines on outer lip near base. Attains 115 mm in length.

5. Phalium strigatum GMELIN. Restricted to South-east Asia. Similar in form to *P. areola*. A white shell, attractively coloured with wavy axial yellow to brown stripes. Average length 75 mm.

6 and 7. Phalium glabratum DUNKER. Dredged from 120 metres off Queensland coast. An uncommon deep-water shell; narrow, thin and glossy; juveniles often transparent; coloured white to cream, some specimens with a row of yellow-brown blotches on whorl below suture, and with a rose to brown zone on the upper dorsal surface. Average length 50 mm.

8. Phalium thomsoni BRAZIER. Dredged 110 metres off mid-Queensland coast. A temperate water species ranging, in the form illustrated, to central Queensland, in deep water. Uncommon. A thin shell for its size; flesh coloured, with rows of indistinct brown blotches; three to five spiral grooves near base, and numerous longitudinal folds or wrinkles; row of fine axially elongate nodules at shoulder. Average length 65 mm.

9. Morum cancellatum SOWERBY. Known from the China Seas, and the east coast of Australia. Figured specimen from 75 metres, mid-Queensland coast. An attractive deep yellow to orange form of 65 mm. A scarce shell.

10. Morum cancellatum SOWERBY. Typical form which is white with four indistinct spiral bands of brown. Twelve widely-spaced, raised spiral ridges are crossed by eighteen axial ribs, resulting in a spinous development at the intersections. An unusual and attractive pattern. Uncommon. Averages 65 mm.

11. Phalium bisulcatum SCHUBERT & WAGNER. Dredged 22 metres west coast of Bougainville Island. Distribution Indo-Pacific. An extremely variable species which has caused much confusion and synonymy. Cream, with six spiral rows of squarish brown blotches, and a thin line between; spire and base deeply grooved; smooth on central section of body whorl. Average length 45 mm.

12. Phalium bisulcatum sophia BRAZIER. A subspecies occurring in deep water off mid-Queensland coast. More globose than previous form. A smooth, light-weight, white shell, with five rows of small evenly and widely spaced light brown squarish spots. Uncommon. Average length 55 mm.

13. Phalium bisulcatum SCHUBERT & WAGNER. Dredged 33 metres, Gulf of Papua. A thin shell, more elongate than previous forms. White, with five rows of yellow-brown blotches, not well defined and absent in some specimens. A rose-coloured blotch on upper dorsal surface. Whole of whorl with evenly spaced fine spiral grooves. Not common. To 65 mm.

14 and 15. Cassis nana TENISON-WOODS. Trawled from prawn grounds to 180 metres depth off south Queensland. Uncommon. A flesh-coloured shell, with four spiral bands of alternating white and brown; the bands are noduled, becoming spinose at shoulder. An attractive little cassid averaging 45 mm in length.

16. Phalium labiatum PERRY. Normally a cool water species, races found in South Africa, South America and South Australia, but this form ranges into the warmer seas of the tropical Indo-Pacific, being taken in prawn trawl nets to 140 metres off mid-Queensland coast. Off-white to cream with reddish-brown blotches and spots below suture, and occasional irregular blotches on whorl. A smooth shell with the exception of two rows of weak nodules, one at shoulder and the other slightly below. Averages 50 mm.

17 and 18. Casmaria erinaceus LINNE. A variable species with a wide distribution throughout the Indo-Pacific. Forms with smooth shoulders and others with heavy nodules are found in the one population. The figured specimen from Trobriand Islands is the typical nodulose form. A character common to all forms is the presence of five or six small but well-defined sharp spines on the lower outer section of lip. A common species from 40 to 75 mm in length.

19. Casmaria erinaceus LINNE. Trobriand Islands. Smooth form marked with axial wavy lines. Average length 60 mm.

20. Casmaria erinaceus LINNE. Another variety from Trobriand Islands, with oddly thickened lip.

21. Casmaria ponderosa GMELIN. Yule Island, Papua. Distribution — Indo-Pacific. A smaller shell and less abundant than previous species with which it is often confused. Has a row of reddish-brown spots below suture, and one or two rows at base. A row of small sharp spines extends full length of aperture. As with *C. erinaceus*, both smooth and nodulose forms occur in this species. Averages 40 mm.

22. Casmaria ponderosa GMELIN. Form with nodulose shoulder and less produced spire. Figured specimen dredged from 65 metres off mid-Queensland coast.

23. Casmaria ponderosa. GMELIN. This species from Manus Island appears stunted, with a thickened lip and peristome, greatly reducing the size of the aperture. In this almost grotesque form, the usual rows of spots are often obsolete, and this shell often appears in collections with *C. erinaceus*. (See No. 20, this plate.) However, the row of fine spines running the full length of the outer lip is a differentiating feature.

PLATE 8
1
2
3
4
5
6
7
8
9
10
11
12
13
14
15
16
17
18
19
20
21
22
23

FAMILY TONNIDAE. The tuns, closely related to the cassids, are generally thin textured, large, globular shells, with a greatly inflated body whorl, and wide aperture. They are carnivorous; lack an operculum; and the shell is covered in life with a thin papery epidermis. An attractive shell for ornamental purposes, and popular for making into reading lamps.

1. **Tonna allium** DILLWYN. Dredged from 9 metres, Yule Island, Gulf of Papua. Distribution — central Indo-Pacific. Reasonably common offshore in 10 to 20 metres. A white shell with smooth, narrow, light brown ribs, widely and evenly spaced. Average length 75 mm.
2. **Tonna canaliculata** LINNE. Trobriand Islands. Distribution — Indo-Pacific. Uncommon. Intertidal to a few metres depth. A shiny brown shell, with some irregular white and dark brown blotches. Ribs are wide and flat, with a narrow groove between. Sutures deeply channelled. Average length 75 mm.
3. **Tonna canaliculata** LINNE. Ventral view.
4. **Tonna perdix** LINNE. Port Moresby. A common species in north Australia, New Guinea and throughout the tropical Indo-Pacific. Prefers grass- and weed-covered intertidal lagoon areas, close to coral reefs. A large elongate shell attaining 130 mm. Brown, with broad flat ribs ornamented with white crescent or chevron shaped bars.
5. **Tonna chinensis** DILLWYN. Trobriand Islands. Distribution — central Indo-Pacific. Not common. A yellowish-brown shell with flattened ribs ornamented with alternate white and brown dashes. Average length 75 mm.
6. **Tonna tessellata** LAMARCK. Taken in prawn trawl nets in 5 to 10 metres from sand or mud bottom in Gulf of Papua. Distribution — Indo-Pacific. Uncommon. An attractive tun shell, grey to cream, with about fourteen narrow flattened ribs ornamented with reddish-brown and white spots and dashes. The wide spaces between ribs with one to three fine intermediate ribs and grooves. Averages 65 mm.
7. **Tonna sulcosa** BORN. Trobriand Islands. Distribution — central Indo-Pacific. From intertidal sand flats to about 30 metres. Attains 100 mm and larger. A white shell with a narrow spiral ribbing, widely spaced near shoulder, becoming more crowded approaching the base. Spiral bands of light brown vary in number and width from specimen to specimen. Uncommon.
8. **Tonna sulcosa** BORN. Dorsal view.
9. **Malea pomum** LINNE. Siassi Islands, west New Britain. Distribution — central Indo-Pacific. Uncommon. A solid glossy shell, with twelve to fourteen smooth flattened ribs; white, attractively ornamented with irregular blotches of orange, brown and mauve. Columella and lip white, the latter thickened, and with ten to twelve raised teeth extending into aperture. Average length 50 mm.
10. **Malea pomum** LINNE. Ventral view.

FAMILY FICIDAE. The fig shells are thin, of medium size, and fig- or pear-shaped. They have an extremely large body whorl, narrowing anteriorly. Related to the Tonnidae.

11. **Ficus subintermedia** *D'Orbigny* In prawn trawl nets from 20 metres, Gulf of Papua. Distribution — Indo-Pacific. Reasonably common off-shore. A fine pear-shaped shell of a cream colour, with five or six narrow bands blotched with brown. Fine spiral ribs and finer longitudinal raised lines causing a coarse but attractive granulated pattern. Average length 75 mm.
12. **Ficus ficus** LINNE. Dredged 15 metres, Wewak, New Guinea. Distribution — Indo-Pacific. Reasonably common. More inflated and wider than previous species. Cream to light brown, densely and irregularly marked with dark brown. Aperture mauve to deep purple. Average length 75 mm.

PLATE 9
1
2
3
4
5
6
7
8
9
10
11
12

FAMILY CYPRAEIDAE. The colourful and highly polished cowries are so well known and admired that a description is not necessary. They are probably the most popular group of marine gastropods with shell collectors, and are a natural favourite with travellers seeking a memento of happy days spent on a tropical beach. Though variable from species to species, the typical cowries are distinct from all other marine shells, with the exception of the allied cowries of the family Ovulidae. However, the amateur collector should have little difficulty if he uses one simple shell characteristic to separate the members of these related families. All representatives of the true cowries, occuring in the central Indo-Pacific, are strongly toothed on both sides of the aperture, whereas the members of the family Ovulidae are denticulate, sometimes strongly, on the outer (labial) lip, but smooth on the inner (columella) lip. The juvenile or "bulla" stage is so different in form to the adult cowry that it is often difficult to identify a juvenile specimen. In the "bulla" form, the cowry is a typically coiled snail, with a very frail outer lip, and with the general shape of a volute. The lavishly-spotted adult species are often multi-banded in a spiral pattern in the juvenile stages. A growth series of a species is most interesting, and serious collectors attempt to include these variations in their cabinet. Collectors specializing in the family Cypraeidae are keen to display variable forms or races that are sometimes quite distinct over a wide distribution range. This certainly makes a collection more interesting. Many subspecies have been named, and it is regrettable to see the original author's names disappearing from check lists. In the following plates and relative text depicting and describing the Cypraeidae, splitting to subspecific level has been purposely avoided. However, the locality of each specimen illustrated is quoted to permit the serious collector or researcher to classify at his or her own discretion. In recent years, anatomical studies of the cowry mollusc have caused a great deal of reshuffling of the many genera. Taxonomy follows that of Burgess, C. M. *The Living Cowrie*, A. S. Barnes & Co. Inc. 1970.

1. **Cypraea argus** LINNE. Samarai, Papua. Distribution — Indo-Pacific. Attractive and uncommon. Elongate and cylindrical; grey or cream with three brown spiral bands; dorsal surface ornamented with large and small brown rings. Base unspotted, but with two large dark brown blotches on the columella, often extending across the aperture to the labial side giving appearance of four blotches. Teeth reddish-brown and short. Average length 75 mm.
2. **Cypraea argus** LINNE. Ventral view.
3. **Cypraea aurantium** GMELIN. Duke of York Islands, New Britain — now in Museum and Art Gallery, Port Moresby. A rare and much prized cowry with a limited range from Philippines and New Guinea in the western Pacific to Polynesia. An evenly inflated and rounded shell; dorsum orange; base white; teeth are short and etched in similar colour as on dorsum. Average length 100 mm.
4. **Cypraea lynx** LINNE. Port Moresby. Distribution — abundant throughout the Indo-Pacific. An ovate shell, cream with an ashy blue overlaying tint; a few large dark brown spots with minute brown maculations and spots. Base white to cream; teeth short but strong; interstices orange-red. Average length 45 mm.
5. **Cypraea lynx** LINNE. Ventral view.
6. **Cypraea carneola** LINNE. Port Moresby. Distribution — Indo-Pacific. An ovate shell, of a reddish-brown colour, with four darker spiral bands. No other markings. Base cream to fawn; teeth short, mostly confined to aperture; interstices a delicate mauve. Average length 45 mm, but odd specimens occur in certain areas to double this size.
7. **Cypraea carneola** LINNE. Ventral view.
8. **Cypraea ventriculus** LAMARCK. Aramot Island, west New Britain. Distribution — limited range from Philippines and New Guinea, through Melanesia to Polynesia. Rare in New Guinea waters, uncommon elsewhere. A broad heavy shell; upper half of dorsum light reddish-brown obsoletely banded in adult specimens; lower part of dorsum and sides a dark brown with fine hair-like lirae. Base fawn to cream; short strong white teeth with interstices reddish-brown inside aperture on central section of columella side only. Average length 50 mm.
9. **Cypraea vitellus** LINNE. Port Moresby, Papua, where this cowry is possibly the most abundant of the larger attractive species. Distribution — throughout the Indo-Pacific. Ovate; dorsum cream to reddish-brown, irregularly ornamented with large and small white spots. On the sides the spots are sometimes raised. Base white to pinkish-mauve, with fine hairlike lines extending well onto dorsal surface. Teeth short and white. Average length 65 mm.
10. **Cypraea vitellus** LINNE. Ventral view.
11. **Cypraea guttata** GMELIN. Figured specimen collected alive on east coast of Bougainville Island. This beautiful and very rare cowry is in the private collection of Mr and Mrs Fred Kleckham of Port Moresby. Inflated and pyriform; dorsum fawn, spotted with white. Most distinctive feature of this shell is the extension of the red teeth across the margins onto the dorsal surface. Little is known of the distribution of this species, as so few specimens have been collected; Melanesia generally with New Britain or Bougainville possibly the centre of a limited range. To 65 mm.

Cowries are herbivores, feeding by night, and spending the hours of daylight hidden under stones, in rock crevices and in coral. Most are shallow-water dwellers, preferring the intertidal coral reefs and lagoons of the tropical seas. A few are from moderately deep water and taken only by diving or dredging. These species are, naturally, the hardest to procure in choice live condition. The large colourful forms are generally quite common when their favoured habitat is found, but some are very rare. The rarity of some species, plus the popularity of the cowry as a colourful display specimen, has created a lucrative market for dealers and some island people.

PLATE 10
1
2
3
4
5
6
7
8
9
10
11

FAMILY CYPRAEIDAE — continued.

1. **Cypraea caputserpentis** LINNE. Abundant throughout New Guinea and the Indo-Pacific, occurs in the temperate waters of the south-east coast of Australia. A heavy shell; depressed; margins splayed; centre of dorsum brown ornamented with cream spots. Chocolate-brown on lower dorsum, continuing partially on to basal periphery. Average length 40 mm.

2. **Cypraea caputserpentis** LINNE. Ventral view.

3. **Cypraea caputserpentis** LINNE. Juvenile specimen lacking angular margins of adult shell.

4. **Cypraea erosa** LINNE. Port Moresby. Distribution — Indo-Pacific. A common species. Heavy; margins splayed and pitted; dorsum fawn, densely sprinkled with small white spots. Sides with a squarish brown to purplish blotch; teeth large, extending across base and over margin on labial side. Average length 40 mm.

5. **Cypraea erosa** LINNE. Ventral view.

6. **Cypraea coxeni** COX. New Britain. Distribution — restricted to New Guinea and Solomon Is. Uncommon. A small, narrow shell, solid for its size. Specimens from Bougainville are heavier and broader than those from New Guinea and New Britain. A white shell, dorsum marked, with irregular and distorted brown figurations; sides and base white. Average length 25 mm.

7. **Cypraea coxeni.** COX. Ventral view.

8. **Cypraea miliaris** GMELIN. Daru, western Papua. Distribution — central Indo-Pacific. Reasonably common. Pyriform, margins grooved. Dorsum fawn to blue-grey, profusely spotted with off-white. Base white, teeth strong. Average length 40 mm.

9. **Cypraea miliaris** GMELIN. Ventral view.

10. **Cypraea miliaris** GMELIN. A colourful form dredged from 20 metres near Samarai, eastern Papua.

11. **Cypraea chinensis** GMELIN. Port Moresby. Distribution — Indo-Pacific. Uncommon. Heavy shell, labial margin angulate; dorsum cream, reticulated with brown. Deep mauve spotting on sides and over margins to base. Aperture wide, teeth strong; interstices orange. Averages 40 mm.

12. **Cypraea chinensis** GMELIN. Ventral view.

13. **Cypraea quadrimaculata** GRAY. Port Moresby. Distribution — restricted to central Indo-Pacific. Uncommon species. Shell narrow ovate; dorsum ash-white sprinkled with brown. Extremities with a pair of bold dark brown spots; sides and base white. Average length 25 mm.

14. **Cypraea pallidula** GASKOIN. Port Moresby. Distribution — central Indo-Pacific to Fiji. Not common. Cylindrical and slightly depressed. Dorsum blue-grey, sprinkled with minute green and brown spots, and has four spiral bands. Base white. To 25 mm.

15. **Cypraea pallidula** GASKOIN. Ventral view.

16. **Cypraea eburnea** BARNES. New Britain. Distribution — New Guinea and north Australia to Fiji. Common along New Guinea coast, but less common elsewhere. In shape and shell characteristics is hardly separable from *C. miliaris*, but recognized as a "good" species by taxonomists. A pure white shell, though occasional specimens occur with a golden-fawn crown to the dorsum. To 50 mm.

17. **Cypraea hirundo** LINNE. New Hebrides. Distribution — Indo-Pacific. Uncommon. Identification of this small cowry is confusing to the amateur collector, and hard to separate from the related species *C. kieneri* and *C. ursellus*. To help overcome this problem, the three species are dealt with collectively and comparatively. With assistance of a magnifying glass, they are easily separated. *C. hirundo* is sub-cylindrical; *C. kieneri* is ovate and slightly depressed; *C. ursellus* is pyriform. In *C. hirundo* and *C. ursellus* the dorsum pattern consists of three broad blue-grey spiral bands, reasonably defined. In *C. kieneri* the three bands or zones are darker and of a very irregular and wayward pattern. The teeth are a further key to identification. In *C. hirundo* the teeth are produced evenly almost to the margins. In *C. kieneri* the teeth on the columella side are short anteriorly but extend to the margin posteriorly. In *C. ursellus* the teeth extend nearly to margins, and well over the margins at posterior extremity. *C. hirundo* attains 20 mm.

18. **Cypraea hirundo** LINNE. Ventral view.

19. **Cypraea ursellus** GMELIN. New Britain. Distribution — western and central Pacific. Uncommon. Averages 15 mm. For description, see under *C. hirundo*.

20. **Cypraea ursellus** GMELIN. Ventral view.

21. **Cypraea kieneri** HIDALGO. Port Moresby. Distribution — Indo-Pacific. Uncommon. 14 to 20 mm. For description, see under *C. hirundo*.

22. **Cypraea kieneri** HIDALGO. Ventral view.

23. **Cypraea boivinii** KIENER. Philippines. Distribution — South-east Asia, Indonesia, and Philippines. Uncommon. Dorsum grey, ornamented with brown spots. Margins pitted, base white. Average length 25 mm.

24. **Cypraea teres** GMELIN. Trobriand Is., eastern Papua. Distribution — Indo-Pacific. Reasonably common. Shell cylindrical; depressed; labial margin angulate; dorsum blue-grey, flecked with brown, and with three spiral bands broken into a chevron pattern. Teeth fine and numerous. Average length 30 mm.

25. **Cypraea teres** GMELIN. Ventral view.

26. **Cypraea stolida** LINNE. Solomon Islands. Distribution — Indo-Pacific. An uncommon and attractive species, variable over its range with many subsequent subspecies named. A series of the race variations make an interesting and beautiful display. The figured specimen is ovate; dorsum cream to grey, with divided central patch of reddish-brown, and four broken lines of same colour curving towards extremities. Very attractive form. Averages 25 mm.

27 and 28. Cypraea brevidentata SOWERBY. **Port Moresby. Distribution — north-west Australia to south Papuan coast. Uncommon. Pyriform; ends slightly produced; dorsum variable in colour from fawn to pink or ash-blue, with reddish-brown blotch. The teeth are less prominent than in *C. stolida*. Average length 30 mm.**

29. **Cypraea stolida** LINNE Juvenile form. Port Moresby.

30. **Cypraea catholicorum** SCHILDER & SCHILDER. Bougainville. Distribution — New Britain to New Caledonia. Rare. A small light cowry, ovate; dorsum yellow to tan, ornamented with clear white spots. To 20 mm.

31. **Cypraea cribraria** LINNE. Samarai, eastern Papua. Distribution — Indo-Pacific. Uncommon. Shell ovate; dorsum reddish-brown, strikingly ornamented with white spots. Average length 30 mm. Occurs in an all-white albinistic form on mid-Queensland coast.

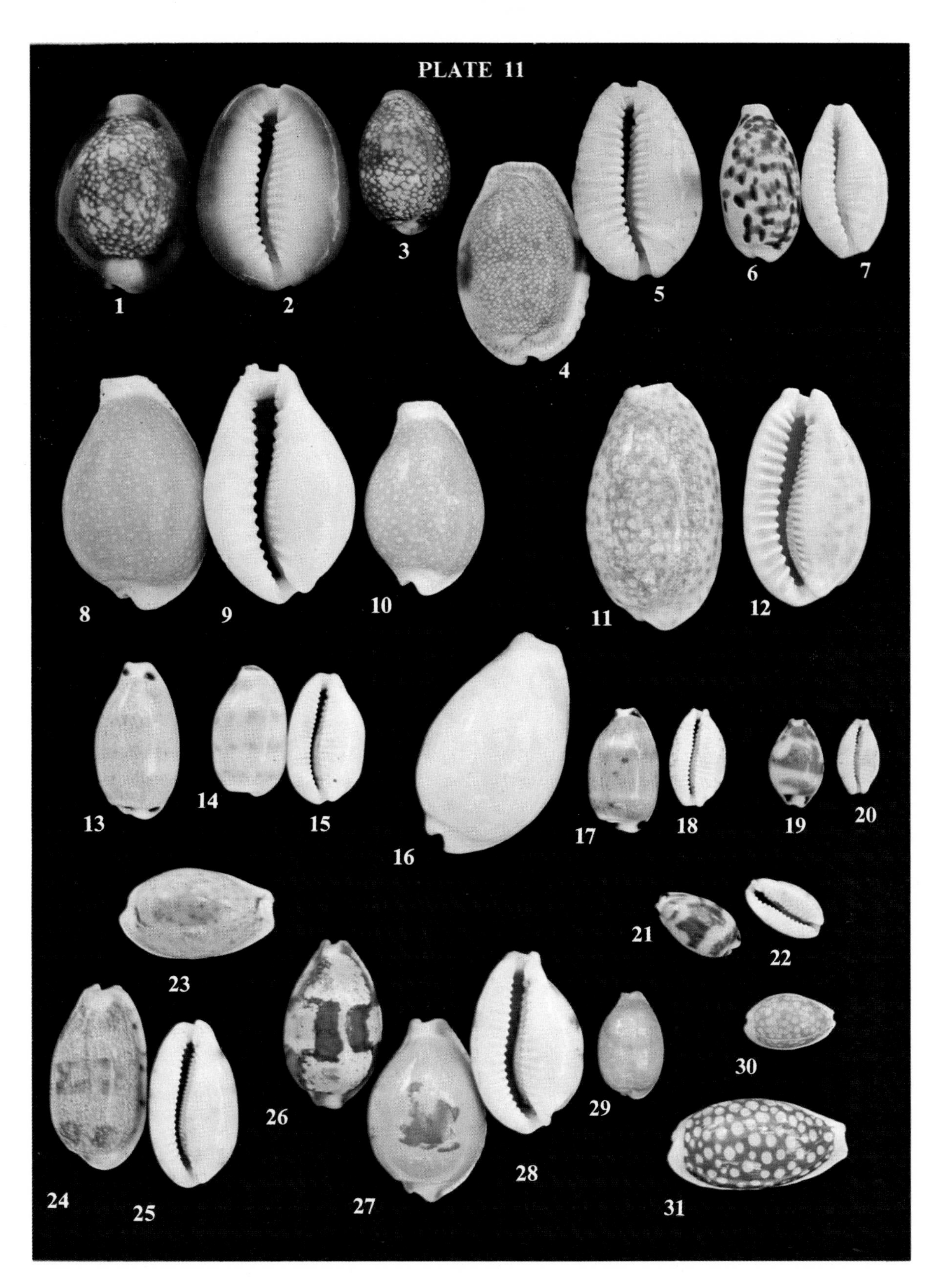
PLATE 11
1
2
3
4
5
6
7
8
9
10
11
12
13
14
15
16
17
18
19
20
21
22
23
24
25
26
27
28
29
30
31

FAMILY CYPRAEIDAE — continued.

1. **Cypraea arabica** LINNE. South Papuan coast. Common. Distribution — Indo-Pacific. The shell is solid, with a broad base; the dorsum irregularly ornamented with longitudinal dark brown lines broken by dots and patches of blue-grey. Teeth reddish-brown and strong. Average length 65 mm, but attains 75 mm and more.
2. **Cypraea arabica** LINNE. Ventral view.
3. **Cypraea arabica** LINNE. Juvenile or bulla stage.
4. **Cypraea eglantina** DUCLOS. South Papuan coast, sharing habitat with *C. arabica*. Not as widely distributed as previous species — western and central Pacific. Of cylindrical shape with rounded sides. 50 to 75 mm in length.
5. **Cypraea eglantina** DUCLOS. Ventral view.
6. **Cypraea eglantina** DUCLOS. Semi-juvenile with the colour pattern distinctly banded.
7. **Cypraea depressa** GRAY. Bougainville Island. Distribution — Indo-Pacific, but not common. A solid shell, almost circular in shape. Brown in colour, with small white spots often merging; sides callused and heavily spotted. Teeth short at centre, longer at both anterior and posterior ends of aperture. A small shell, and more depressed than following species. 30 to 50 mm.
8. **Cypraea maculifera** SCHILDER. Guam. Distribution — Pacific, and reasonably common. A heavy shell, less broad than preceding species; pyriform to humped; whitish spots of variable sizes well defined. A large dark blotch on columella side of aperture is a consistent characteristic in adult specimens. Attains 75 mm.
9. **Cypraea histrio** GMELIN. North-west Australia. Distribution — Indian Ocean to west Australia. A large shell, less solid than *C. maculifera* and *C. depressa*. Clearly defined large greyish-white and odd-shaped spots on dorsal surface, with a straight narrow sulcus, and prominent, wide, brown, underlying spiral band. Teeth short and of comparatively equal length; base cream to pink. 50 to 75 mm.
10. **Cypraea mauritiana** LINNE. Trobriand Islands, Papua. Distribution — Indo-Pacific. A large, heavy, humped shell, and very glossy. Dark brown with large irregular yellow to light brown spots only on dorsum proper; sides and base unspotted; teeth short and strong; interstices offwhite. Average length 90 mm, but grows larger.
11. **Cypraea mauritiana** LINNE. Semi-juvenile form.
12. **Cypraea mauritiana** LINNE. Form from Milne Bay with a red overlay often seen in cowries collected near wrecks of iron vessels.
13. **Cypraea scurra** GMELIN. New Britain. Distribution — Indo-Pacific. Not common. Narrow and cylindrical, mid-brown; dorsum with large grey spots interspersed with minute spots and reticulation; sides rounded and heavily spotted. Teeth short and reddish-brown; aperture narrow and straight. 30 to 50 mm.
14. **Cypraea scurra** GMELIN. Ventral view.
15. **Cypraea mappa** LINNE. Samarai, eastern Papua. Distribution — throughout tropical Indo-Pacific. Uncommon. A popular collector's item. The unusually branched and conspicuous sulcus or dorsal line readily identifies this species. Fawn to brown with fine darker longitudinal lines and odd spots. Base fawn, pink, mauve or occasionally pale green. Aperture narrow; teeth fine and short; usually with purplish blotch on columella side of aperture. A really lovely shell. To 90 mm.
16. **Cypraea testudinaria** LINNE. Trobriand Islands. Distribution — throughout Indo-Pacific. Uncommon. A fawn shell ornamented with dark brown spots and blotches; dusted with very fine white spots. A large cowry, narrow and elongate; aperture narrow and teeth very short. Attains 125 mm.
17. **Cypraea testudinaria** LINNE. Juvenile form.
18. **Cypraea talpa** LINNE. Hula, south Papuan coast. Distribution — Indo-Pacific. Uncommon. A cylindrical shell; dorsum yellow to brown, crossed by four wide darker brown bands; sides chocolate-brown; aperture narrow, teeth short. Averages 65 mm.
19. **Cypraea talpa** LINNE. Ventral view.
20. **Cypraea talpa** LINNE. Large dark form from Rabaul, New Britain.
21. **Cypraea tigris** LINNE. Juvenile (bulla) form. Port Moresby.
22. **Cypraea tigris** LINNE. Semi-adult form. Port Moresby.
23. **Cypraea tigris** LINNE. Port Moresby. Distribution — throughout Indo-Pacific. A common species. Large shell, swollen ovate; of variable colour pattern, but typically white; heavily and irregularly marked with large brown spots. Base white; teeth short but strong. Average length 90 mm, but giant specimens in excess of 130 mm have been recorded.
24. **Cypraea tigris** LINNE. Port Moresby. Dark form. This common cowry varies considerably in depth of colour markings and in density of spots. Specimens with pure white, and others with nearly black, dorsal surfaces are found rarely, and much prized by collectors.

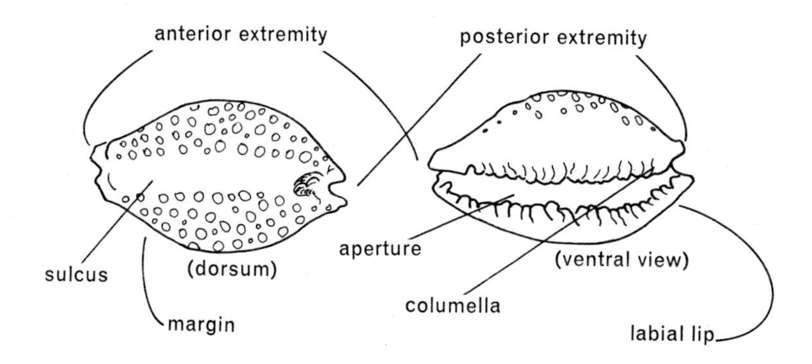

PLATE 12
1
2
3
4
5
6
7
8
9
10
11
12
13
14
15
16
17
18
19
20
21
22
23
24

FAMILY CYPRAEIDAE — continued.

1 and 2. Cypraea isabella LINNE. Hula, south Papuan coast. Distribution — Indo-Pacific. Reasonably common. Shell cylindrical; dorsum fawn or greyish with faint spiral bands and dark brown longitudinal broken lines and dashes; extremities reddish; base white; teeth fine and numerous. Average length 30 mm.

3 and 4. Cypraea moneta LINNE. Madang, New Guinea. Distribution — Indo-Pacific. Common. Very solid shell; depressed with margins expanded. Dorsum white to yellow with obscure spiral bands; base white; teeth short but strong. Average length 30 mm.

5 and 6. Cypraea annulus LINNE. Port Moresby. Distribution — Indo-Pacific. Very common. A heavy ovate shell, slightly depressed. Dorsum grey to cream; crown circled with a deep yellow ring. Aperture white. Average length 25 mm.

7 and 8. Cypraea felina GMELIN. Yule Island, Papua. Distribution — Indo-Pacific. Reasonably common. Cylindrical and slightly depressed; dorsum green to grey, profusely flecked with brown, and with three to four narrow pale bands; sides with large brown spots. Average length 20 mm.

9 and 10. Cypraea caurica LINNE. Port Moresby. Distribution — Indo-Pacific. Common. Ovate and depressed; some race forms are cylindrical. A heavy shell; dorsum cream to pale green, profusely ornamented with small brown spots, and three spiral bands; sides with heavy brown spots; base cream; teeth large, interstices orange. Average length 40 mm.

11 and 12. Cypraea cylindrica BORN. Port Moresby. Distribution — western Pacific. Uncommon. A light shell; narrow and cylindrical; dorsum blue-grey, with one or two lighter spiral bands, and thickly mottled with fine brown flecks; usually with dark central dorsal blotch, often broken as in figured specimen; extremities with a pair of purplish-brown blotches. Average length 30 mm.

13 and 14. Cypraea ovum GMELIN. Madang, New Guinea. Distribution is restricted to central Indo-Pacific, where it is common. Pyriform; dorsum cream to dark olive, profusely flecked with brown, and obscurely banded; sides and base cream to burnt-orange; teeth short, interstices orange. Figured specimen is a handsome dark form not uncommon on the north coast of New Guinea. Average length 40 mm.

15 and 16. Cypraea errones. LINNE. Daru, western Papua. Distribution — central Indo-Pacific. A common and variable species. Cylindrical; dorsum cream to bluish-grey, profusely freckled with brown, and with three spiral bands sometimes obscure; with or without dorsal blotch. Aperture wide at anterior end. Average length, 30 mm.

17. Cypraea errones LINNE. Colour variation from Broome, north-west Australia. Another species with several "race" or subspecific names proposed. Splitting would appear justified when comparing the shells illustrated here, but a large series from the Papuan coast will include these colour variants and intergrading forms.

18 and 19. Cypraea subviridis REEVE. Daru, western Papua. Distribution — south Papuan coast, north and east Australia to New Caledonia. Moderately common in north-east Queensland, uncommon elsewhere. Shell pyriform; dorsum cream to pale grey, freckled with brown. Usually has a brown dorsal blotch, sometimes with a wide interrupted central band. Average length 40 mm.

20 and 21. Cypraea pulchella SWAINSON. Figured specimen from deep water off Taiwan. Distribution — central Indo-Pacific. A rare and colourful species. Shell pyriform; dorsum white, darker at crown, profusely freckled with light brown and spiral rows of dots often obscured by large reddish-brown patches; sides with large brown spots; base white to cream; teeth produced across base on columella side, and vividly coloured in reddish-brown. Average length 40 mm. Forma *novaebrittaniae* Schilder & Schilder, from New Britain and eastern Papua, is smaller than the typical form, and very rare.

22 and 23. Cypraea pyriformis GRAY. South Papuan coast. Distribution — central Indo-Pacific. Uncommon. Pyriform; dorsum cream, flecked with brown, and with three interrupted wide spiral bands; sides spotted; base white to cream; teeth white and restricted to aperture on labial side, but reddish-brown and more produced on columella. Average length 40 mm.

24 and 25. Cypraea walkeri SOWERBY. Philippines. Distribution — central Indo-Pacific. Uncommon. Shell ovate; dorsum cream, profusely flecked with brown, and with central spiral band of brown often broken into chevron-like markings; teeth very fine, interstices violet. Average length 25 mm.

26. Cypraea bregeriana CROSSE. Dredged 40 metres. Samarai, eastern Papua. Distribution — New Guinea to Fiji. Rare in live condition. Shell subpyriform; dorsal surface cream to fawn, minutely and profusely freckled with light brown, further ornamented with one wide and two flanking narrow spiral bands of orange-brown; base pinkish in juvenile specimens, rich nut-brown in adults, often with a darker blotch on columella side of aperture. Average length 25 mm.

27 and 28. Cypraea xanthodon SOWERBY. Appears restricted to Queensland coast where it is reasonably common. A pyriform shell; dorsal surface bluish-grey, minutely freckled with brown, and broadly banded with two or three darker zones; base cream, tinged with orange; sides spotted. Average length 40 mm.

29 and 30. Cypraea onyx LINNE. Philippines. Distribution — Indo-Pacific, with distinct "race" variations. The figured specimen, which is reasonably common, is typical of forms from South-east Asia to Philippines. Dorsum usually cream, with two or three darker spiral bands; margins and base rich dark brown; aperture wide anteriorly. Average length 40 mm.

31. Cypraea onyx adusta LAMARCK. The east African form illustrated here to permit comparison with the central Indo-Pacific races.

32 and 33. Cypraea onyx melanesiae SCHILDER & SCHILDER. Dredged 10 fathoms, entrance to Port Moresby Harbour. A moderately rare form, appears to be a deeper-water shell. Distribution — New Guinea to Fiji. A broader and more ovate shell than preceding forms. Glossy dark brown colour, sometimes with reddish-chestnut blotches and zones on dorsal surface; teeth coarse and coloured orange-brown. Averages a little over 25 mm in length.

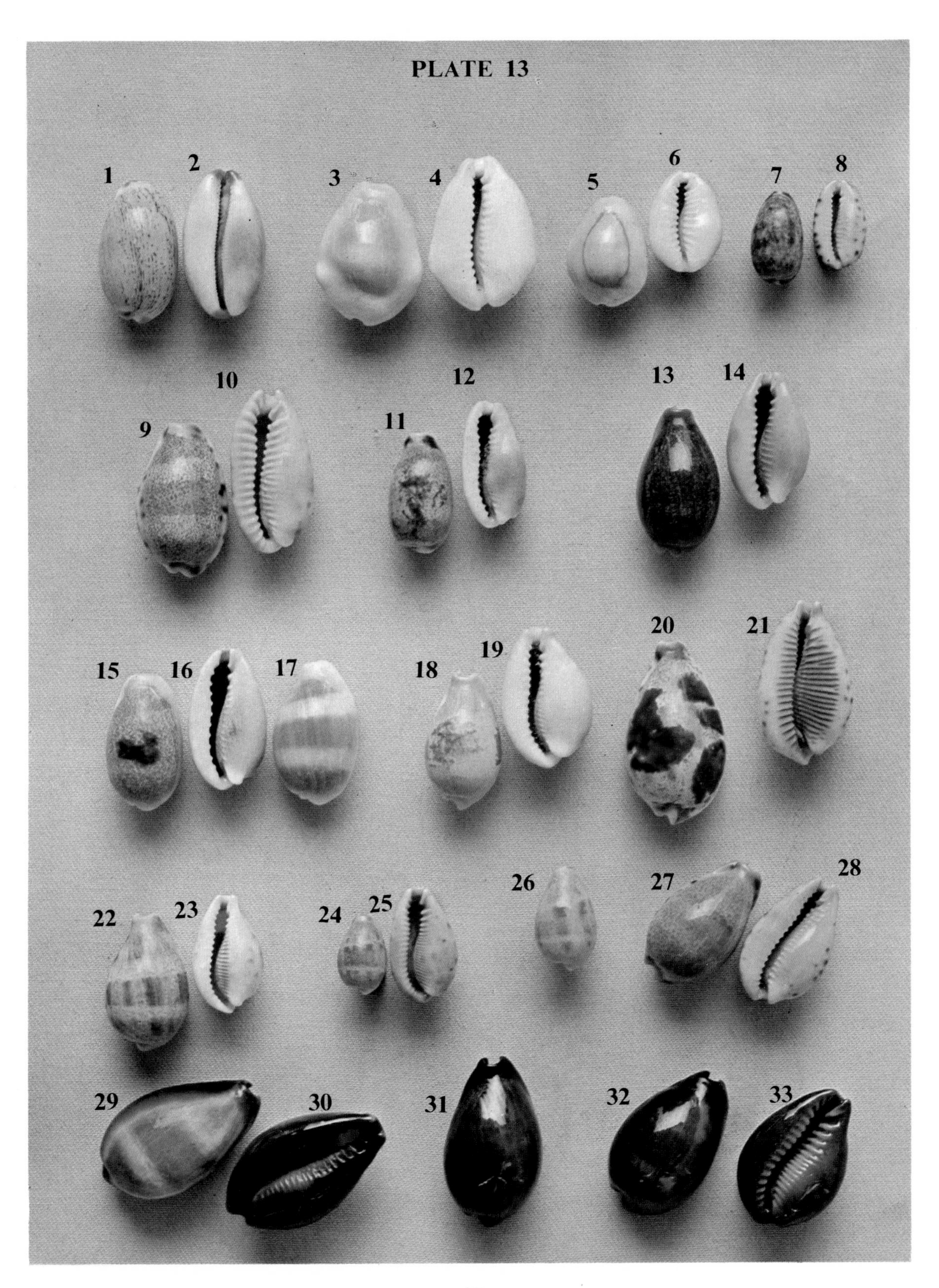
PLATE 13
1
2
3
4
5
6
7
8
9
10
11
12
13
14
15
16
17
18
19
20
21
22
23
24
25
26
27
28
29
30
31
32
33

FAMILY CYPRAEIDAE — continued

1. **Cypraea punctata** LINNE. Samarai, Papua. Distribution — Indo-Pacific. Uncommon. A pretty little cowry, ovate; white; sparsely ornamented with fairly large reddish brown spots which cover all of the dorsal surface and sides and extend partially onto the base. Average length 15 mm.
2. **Cypraea punctata** LINNE. Ventral view.
3. **Cypraea asellus** LINNE. Port Moresby. Distribution — Indo-Pacific. Reasonably common. An ovate, white shell, with three broad dark brown spiral bands. No other markings. Average length 15 mm.
4. **Cypraea asellus** LINNE. Ventral view.
5. **Cypraea clandestina** LINNE. Port Moresby. Distribution — Indo-Pacific. Moderately common. Pyriform; white shell with three fawn or grey dorsal zones, and very fine zigzag lines of light brown. Sides and base white and unspotted. Average length 20 mm.
6. **Cypraea contaminata** SOWERBY. Solomon Islands. Distribution — Indian Ocean to central Indo-Pacific. Uncommon to rare species. A small ovate shell, dorsum cream to grey, ornamented with three wide spiral bands, a wayward central blotch; sides and base spotted. Average length 15 mm.
7. **Cypraea saulae** GASKOIN. Daru, western Papua. Distribution — south-west Pacific. A rare shell. Pyriform and elongated. Dorsum pale grey, with a golden-brown dorsal patch and a few spots on the margins. Length to 25 mm.
8. **Cypraea humphreysii** GRAY. North Queensland. Distribution — Australia and New Guinea to Fiji. Moderately rare. Pyriform shaped; cream to light brown, with three bluish-white spiral bands, spotted on dorsum, sides and base with reddish-brown. Base orange-brown. Average length 20 mm.
9. **Cypraea humphreysii** GRAY. Ventral view.
10. **Cypraea humphreysii** GRAY. A choice, large, and heavily spotted form dredged near Daru, western Papua.
11. **Cypraea lutea** GMELIN. Porebada, Papuan coast. Distribution — central Indo-Pacific. Uncommon. Swollen-ovate; dorsum honey-brown, obscure flecks of darker brown, and two bluish-white spiral bands. Sides heavily spotted. Base orange-brown. Average length 20 mm.
12. **Cypraea ziczac** LINNE. Port Moresby. Distribution — Indo-Pacific. An uncommon and attractive cowry, very popular with collectors. Pyriform shaped; dorsum soft golden-brown, with three spiral bands of unusual chevron-like whitish bars. Base nut-brown; sides and base spotted. Average length 20 mm.
13. **Cypraea irrorata** GRAY. Solomon Islands. Distribution — limited range in central and south-west Pacific. Fairly rare in western Pacific. A small shell, cylindrical and slightly depressed. Dorsum bluish-white with three obscure spiral bands; ornamented with minute brown spots. Average length 20 mm.
14. **Cypraea limacina** LAMARCK. Port Moresby. Distribution — Indo-Pacific. Uncommon. A subpyriform shell, dorsum blue-grey, sparsely ornamented with white spots which tend to be raised approaching the margins; extremities burnt-orange; base off-white; teeth etched with brown. Average length 25 mm.
15. **Cypraea nucleus** LINNE. Port Moresby. Distribution — Indo-Pacific. Uncommon. A heavy ovate shell, of a uniform, unmarked shade of fawn. Only break in colour is the conspicuous, straight dorsal or sulcus line, which is deep and coloured pale blue. Whole of dorsum decorated with raised pustules. The teeth are strong and cross the base. Average length 25 mm.
16. **Cypraea staphylaea** LINNE. Port Moresby. Distribution — Indo-Pacific. Reasonably common. A small roundly ovate shell. Dorsum blue, grey or mauve, covered with raised pustules. Each pustule crowned with white. Extremities are coloured burnt-orange. Teeth extend across base to margins. Average length 20 mm.
17. **Cypraea staphylaea** LINNE. Ventral view.
18. **Cypraea poraria** LINNE. Trobriand Islands. Distribution — Indo-Pacific. Uncommon. An ovate shell; dorsum coloured in mottled shades of brown, with a sprinkling of small cream spots. Sides mauve to violet, the colouring continuing nearly to the white teeth. Average length 20 mm.
19. **Cypraea poraria** LINNE. Ventral view.
20. **Cypraea helvola** LINNE. New Britain. Distribution — Indo-Pacific. This really beautiful little cowry is reasonably common throughout its wide range. A very solid shell, ovate in shape, with margins much expanded. The dorsum crown is pale mauve, profusely spotted with white and dark brown. Mid-dorsum is dark reddish-brown, margins and base burnt-orange. An obscure darker blotch on columella side of aperture. Average length 25 mm.
21. **Cypraea helvola** LINNE. Ventral view.
22. **Cypraea labrolineata** GASKOIN. Philippines. Distribution — central Indo-Pacific to Hawaii. Reasonably common on the Papuan and New Guinea coasts, but less common elsewhere. An elongate shell; dorsum olive-green ornamented with large and small white spots. Margins pitted and sparsely spotted with dark brown. Average length 20 mm.
23. **Cypraea labrolineata** GASKOIN. Ventral view of a specimen from Port Moresby. This form is lighter in colour and more ovate than elongate in shape.
24. **Cypraea cernica** SOWERBY. New Caledonia. Distribution — Indo-Pacific. A rare species. A small solid shell; ovate; dorsum yellow-brown with white to cream spots. Sides lightly spotted; margins and base white. The Melanesian race averages 20 mm.
25. **Cypraea becki** GASKOIN. Philippines. Distribution — has a narrow range band across the Pacific from South-east Asia, Philippines to Hawaii. Rare. A small pyriform shell with extremities slightly produced. Dorsum honey-brown with obscure white spots and a fine sprinkling of clear dark dots which persist partially onto the base periphery. Teeth reddish-brown. Average length 15 mm.

PLATE 14
1
2
3
4
5
6
7
8
9
10
11
12
13
14
15
16
17
18
19
20
21
22
23
24
25

FAMILY CYPRAEIDAE — continued.

1 and 2. Cypraea cicercula LINNE. New Britain. Indo-Pacific range. Uncommon. A small inflated shell; beaked at extremities; dorsum granulated; coloured fawn to grey; aperture straight and narrow; teeth extend across base. Average length 20 mm.

3 and 4. Cypraea bistrinotata SCHILDER & SCHILDER. Samarai, Papua. Indo-Pacific range. Uncommon. A globular, beaked shell; granulated, but less than in previous species; of an ochraceous yellow, with three pairs of spots on dorsum, and four spots on the base. Average length 14 to 20 mm.

5. Cypraea childreni GRAY. New Hebrides. Indo-Pacific range. Scarce. An inflated shell; extremities slightly beaked; yellow-brown, with a small brown blotch above each extremity; teeth strong, extend over the base and margins, becoming spiral ridges over the dorsum, broken only at the narrow sulcus line. Average length 20 mm.

6 and 7. Cypraea globulus LINNE. Solomon Islands. Indo-Pacific range. Uncommon. This species is smooth, and teeth do not extend to margins. Inflated and humped; light brown, spotted on dorsal surface; two pairs of spots on base. Average length 20 mm.

8 and 9. Cypraea margarita DILLWYN. Bougainville Island. Indo-Pacific range. Rare. A humped shell, with extremities produced and beaked; dorsum cream to fawn-grey, sparsely spotted and mottled with brown; aperture narrow; teeth short. A smooth polished cowry. Little over 13 mm. in length.

10 and 11. Cypraea mariae SCHILDER. Solomon Islands. Pacific range. Rare. Of a round bulbous shape; extremities only slightly produced; dorsum white, with fawn spots each ringed with a dark brown ocellation; base white; teeth minute, and confined to the aperture. Average length 16 mm.

12 and 13. Cypraea gracilis GASKOIN. Daru, Papua. Range, Indian Ocean to western Pacific. Uncommon. Subpyriform; dorsum slate-grey, ornamented with brown spots and a central blotch sometimes forming a broken spiral band; sides spotted; base cream; teeth short. Average length 20 mm.

14 and 15. Cypraea hammondae IREDALE. Queensland. Range, Philippines to Australia. Scarce. An ovate shell, expanded at anterior end; white in colour, profusely sprinkled with minute pinkish-brown spots, and larger spots on margins; teeth short. 14 to 20 mm.

16. Cypraea fimbriata GMELIN. Philippines. Indo-Pacific range. Uncommon. Shell elongate-ovate; dorsum blue-grey, faintly flecked with brown, and with two or three brown spiral bands, the central band wider; extremities with pair mauve blotches; base white; teeth short; aperture wide anteriorly. Average length 16 mm.

17 and 18. Cypraea minoridens MELVILL. Port Moresby. Western Pacific range. Uncommon. Ovate, slightly depressed; dorsum honey-brown, finely flecked in brown; two or three spiral bands, centre band usually wider; extremities with pair of mauve to purple terminal blotches; sides and base white; aperture wider anteriorly, but not as wide as with previous species; teeth small. Average length 10 mm.

19. Cypraea microdon GRAY. Siassi Islands. Indo-Pacific range. Rather rare. Very close to previous species, but this small cowry is pyriform shaped, and the aperture is narrow for its full length (both *C. fimbriata* and *minoridens* have a wide aperture anteriorly, particularly the former). Dorsum is pink to pale fawn, very faintly flecked with brown, and three bands of brown maculations; extremities with mauve to purple terminal blotches; base white; teeth very small, mostly restricted to aperture. 10 to 15 mm in length.

FAMILY OVULIDAE. "The allied cowries" lack the regular toothed aperture of the true cowries, usually obsoletely toothed or denticulate on the outer or labial lip, and smooth, occasionally denticulate, on the columella lip. They feed on soft corals.

20. Diminovula bimaculata A. ADAMS. Port Moresby. Range — central Indo-Pacific. Uncommon. Pear shaped; dorsum inflated, white, with three bands of light brown maculations. Averages 14 mm.

21. Prionovolva cavanaghi IREDALE. Queensland. Indo-Pacific range. Uncommon. Pyriform; dorsum swollen, salmon coloured and smooth; base cream. Average length 14 mm.

22. Diminovula pyriformis SOWERBY. White form collected at Rossel Island, eastern Papua. Typical colour form illustrated by No. 24 below.

23. Diminovula punctata DUCLOS. Daru, Papua. Indo-Pacific range. Uncommon. A pyriform shell; dorsum white, with six to nine reddish-brown spots; extremities produced. Averages 10 mm.

24. Diminovula pyriformis SOWERBY. Yule Island, Papua. Indo-Pacific range. Uncommon. Ovate to pyriform; dorsum light brown, with three spiral bands often indistinct; extremities produced and recurved. Average length 20 mm.

25. Prionovolva nubeculata ADAMS & REEVE. Yule Island, Papua. A central Indo-Pacific species with much variation over the range. This form is light, ovate; dorsum pale pink, with three indistinct central zones of light brown; outer lip contrastingly white. Average length 20 mm.

26. Volva volva LINNE. Dredged, Gulf of Papua. Indo-Pacific range. Common offshore. Figured specimen is a juvenile. Adults attain 130 mm and longer.

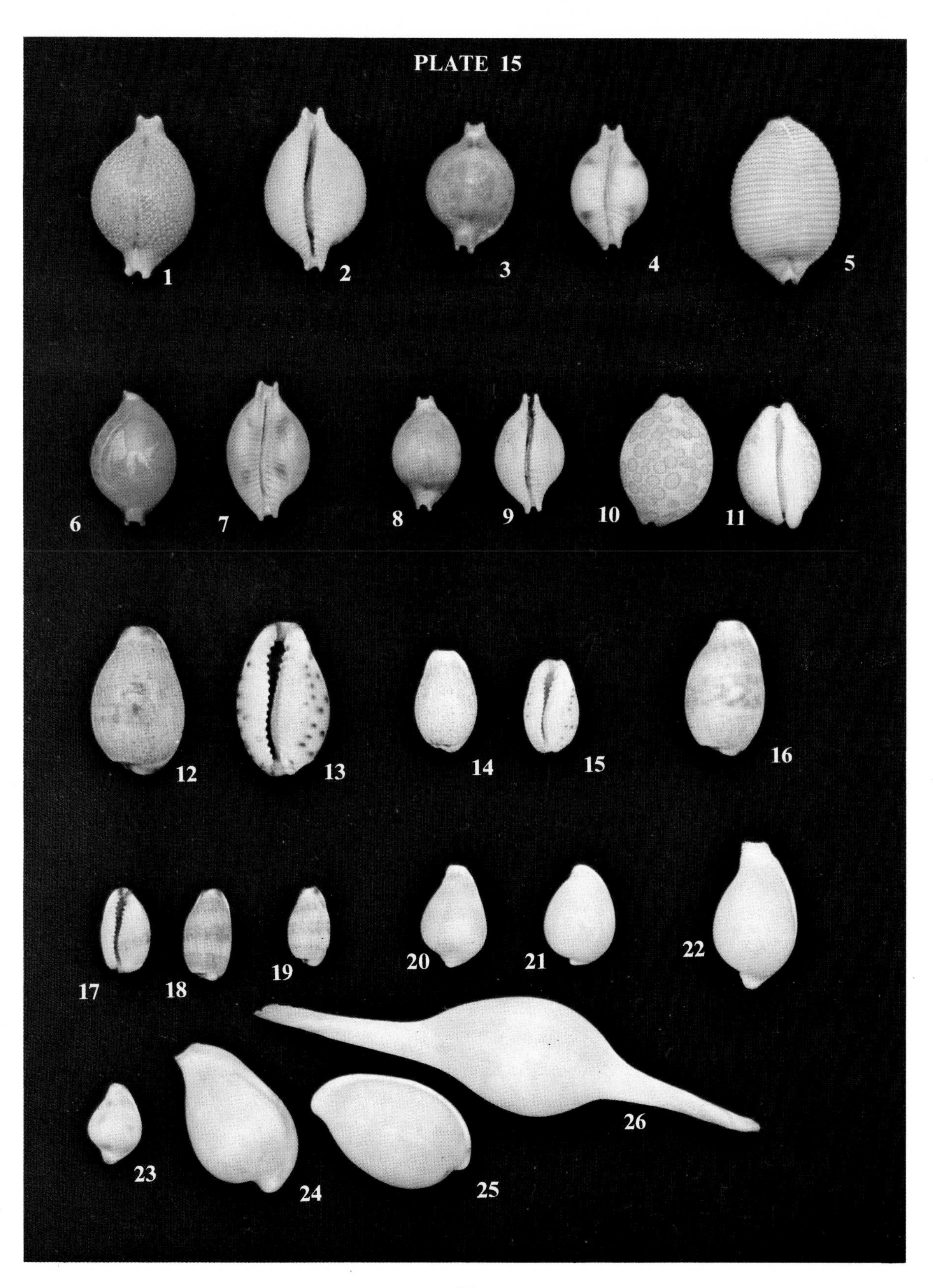
PLATE 15
1
2
3
4
5
6
7
8
9
10
11
12
13
14
15
16
17
18
19
20
21
22
23
24
25
26

FAMILY OVULIDAE — continued.

1. **Calpurnus verrucosus** LINNE. Port Moresby. Distribution — Indo-Pacific. A common species, often found in small colonies on soft corals in shallow water. White and smooth, with a dorsal lateral ridge, and an eyelike granule at each extremity. The ends of aperture tinted pink to mauve. Average length 25 mm.
2. **Ovula costellata** LAMARCK. Samarai, eastern Papua. Distribution — Indo-Pacific. A scarce shell over most of its range. The dorsum is slightly and roundly ridged laterally. This feature, the smaller size, and the pink to mauve colour of interior of shell, readily separate this species from *O. ovum*. Averages 45 mm.
3. **Ovula ovum** LINNE. Samarai, eastern Papua. A common species throughout the Indo-Pacific. Large, white and shiny, interior reddish-brown. Usually found on algae- and weed-covered bottom of coral rubble in 18 to 40 metres of water in lagoons, close to coral reefs. Average length 90 mm.

FAMILY FASCIOLARIIDAE. Includes the large spindle shells with their long anterior canals, and some genera comprising small rugged species a mere 25 mm in length. This family, and all of those following are carnivores.

4. **Saginafusus pricei** SMITH. Taken in prawn trawl nets to 20 metres in Gulf of Papua. Distribution — central Indo-Pacific. Uncommon. A solid shell, of a nut-brown colour, with low spiral ribs a darker shade of brown. About ten spinous nodules at shoulder. Averages 180 mm.
5. **Pleuroploca trapezium** LINNE. Bougainville Island. Distribution — Indo-Pacific. Uncommon. A light brown shell, with numerous fine reddish-brown spiral lines and irregular flat axial grooves. Seven to nine prominent knobs on shoulder. Inside of aperture yellow, crossed by fine red lirae. Average length 100 mm.
6. **Pleuroploca filamentosa** RÖDING. Common on intertidal reefs near Port Moresby. Distribution — Indo-Pacific. A bluish-grey shell with longitudinal streaks and spiral lines of brown. Fine spiral grooves and a row of ten to twelve nodules on shoulder. Interior cream crossed by fine raised brown ridges. Averages 130 mm.
7. **Fusinus colus** LINNE. Siassi Islands, west New Britain. Distribution — Indo-Pacific. A spindle shaped shell with tall spire and long anterior canal. Fine spiral ribs and longitudinal ridges forming nodules at shoulder. A white shell marked with reddish-brown between ridges. Average length 130 mm.
8. **Fusinus salisburyi** FULTON. Dredged 64 metres, off Queensland coast. Uncommon. A large species, similar in form to *F. colus*; the longitudinal ridges on early whorls are mostly limited to prominent nodules on the shoulder of body whorl; colour white, with occasional brown markings restricted to axial folds on the spire. Average length 180 mm.
9. **Fusinus nicobaricus** LAMARCK. Manus Island, Admiralty Group. Distribution — Japan to New Guinea. Appears scarce on its southern range. A white shell profusely marked with small dark brown lines and spots. A rugged shell with coarse spiral ribs and spinous nodules at shoulder. Average length 100 mm.
10. **Fusinus novaehollandae** REEVE. A large deepwater species from east coast of Australia. White, with raised spiral ridges and rounded axial ribs becoming obsolete on body whorl. Average length 180 mm.
11. **Latirus barclayi** REEVE. Dredged Gulf of Papua. Uncommon. A solid shell, with fine spiral ribs and two rows of large rounded nodules on body whorl. White, stained orange-brown between the nodules. Figured specimen 57 mm.
12. **Latirus gibbulus** GMELIN. Siassi Islands, west New Britain, where it is reasonably common. A large, heavy species, light brown in colour, with fine spiral grooves which are coloured dark brown. Usually heavily encrusted with coral, and pitted when cleaned. Averages 75 mm.
13. **Latirulus craticulatus** LINNE. Samarai, eastern Papua. Uncommon. Solid, tall spire and small aperture. Cream coloured, numerous raised spiral ribs and rounded axial ridges, coloured reddish-brown. Average length 60 mm.
14. **Latirulus turritus** GMELIN. Dredged 30 metres, Yule Is., Papua. Distribution — Indo-Pacific. Reasonably common, though seldom collected alive. A stout shell, tall spire, comparatively small aperture. Orange-brown, with fine spiral ribs etched in dark brown to black. Low, broad longitudinal folds. Average length 45 mm.
15. **Peristernia nassatula** LAMARCK. Abundant throughout Papua and New Guinea on intertidal coral reefs. Distribution — Indo-Pacific. An attractive species, with raised spiral beads and axial ridges. A white shell with bands of reddish-brown. Aperture mauve. Average length 40 mm.
16. **Latirolagena smaragdula** LINNE. Port Moresby. Distribution — Indo-Pacific. Solid, ovate, dark brown, with fine spiral ribs and lines of white. Aperture white. Average length 40 mm.

FAMILY BUCCINIDAE. These shells are closely related to the Fasciolariidae.

17. **Penion maxima** TRYON. Taken in prawn trawl nets on mid-Queensland coast southwards. Common. A large, comparatively light shell, cream, with fine spiral ribs and lines of dark brown; angulate and nodulose at shoulder. Average length 200 mm.
18. **Cantharus fumosus** DILLWYN. Yule Island, Papuan coast. Small, solid, yellow-brown, with dark brown curving axial ridges. Fine spiral ribs and a thin white line about centre of whorl. Aperture orange, interior white. Averages 30 mm.
19. **Cantharus undosus** LINNE. Port Moresby. Distribution — Indo-Pacific. Common. Shell solid, ovate; white, with raised spiral ribs of dark brown. Aperture white. Average length 40 mm.
20. **Cantharus fumosus** DILLWYN. White form from Samarai, eastern Papua. See No. 18.
21. **Phos senticosus** LINNE. A common species from intertidal sand and mud flats to 10 metres, throughout Papua and New Guinea. Distribution — Indo-Pacific. A brown shell, irregularly banded, and with fine spiral ribs and raised axial ridges; spinous at shoulder. Average length 40 mm.
22. **Pisania fasciculata** REEVE. Dredged Port Moresby Harbour. Distribution — central Indo-Pacific. Not common. A small smooth and polished shell, cream, with spiral rows of reddish-brown lines and dashes. Average length 30 mm.

PLATE 16
1
2
3
4
5
6
7
8
9
10
11
12
13
14
15
16
17
18
19
20
21
22

FAMILY MURICIDAE. An intricately sculptured group of shells that are characterized by prominent spinous, frilly, or fin-like varices, often creating a most attractive pattern. A fascinating family, usually well represented in the collector's display cabinet. The sizes of the various species are as diversified as their form, ranging from a fraction of an inch to the bulky proportions of the showy Ramosa Murex, which attains 300 mm. The murex shells are carnivores, preying on other molluscs. Some are pests, often multiplying to plague proportions in the vicinity of large commercial oyster leases. The operculum is horny, and fills the aperture. Some species are found on intertidal mangrove roots, others are taken by dredges and prawn trawl nets to depths below 180 metres.

1. **Murex troscheli** LISCHKE. Distribution — Japan to New Guinea, but most abundant over its northern range. The largest of the fish-bone murex, averaging 150 mm. Of a cream colour, with raised brown spiral ribs. Spines long and strong.

2. **Murex pecten** LIGHTFOOT. (=*M. triremis* PERRY.) Dredged 18 metres, Gulf of Papua. Ranges from north Australia to South-east Asia. The most attractive of the spiny forms, with its numerous long and slightly curved spines. Uncommon. Average length 125 mm.

3 and 4. **Murex nigrospinosus** REEVE. A rather scarce shell; figured specimens collected on mud and grass in 4 metres of water in West New Britain. The spines are long and exceptionally strong, and banded dark brown. The anterior canal not as straight as in related species. Average length 100 mm.

5. **Murex coppingeri** E. A. SMITH. Dredged 13 metres, Gulf of Papua. Range unknown; recorded also from north Australia. A rather scarce shell. Cream to fawn, with smooth spiral ribs; angulate at shoulder; two to three longitudinal ridges causing elongate nodules between varices. Solid shell; spines stout, of medium length, and curved. Aperture white. Figured specimen 64 mm.

6. **Murex tribulus** LINNE. Dredged 55 metres, Oro Bay, north coast of Papua. Range — tropical Indo-Pacific. Reasonably common. Extremely variable from locality to locality, but the main shell characters remain reasonably consistent. Most variation occurs in the colour of the shell and aperture, and in the length of spines. This deepwater specimen has a lighter shell than the forms from shallow water, and is not as common. Cream to fawn in colour, body whorl decorated with numerous large and small raised granular ribs; aperture light brown; anterior canal long and thin; spines very long, frail, and sharp. Average length 100 mm.

7. **Murex tribulus** LINNE. Collected from 2 to 4 metres, on mud and grass, west New Britain. A heavier shell than preceding form, spines less produced, and shell of a dark brown colour, with aperture purplish-brown. Common. Average length 100 mm.

8. **Pterynotus bednalli** BRAZIER. Torres Strait to north-west Australia. A rare and beautiful murex. Mostly white, some specimens yellow to cream, with light brown patches. Aperture cream. The fin-like varices are delicately sculptured, but surprisingly are not as fragile as they appear. Figured specimen 76·2 mm.

9. **Murex macgillivrayi** DOHRN. Trawled from 13 metres, Gulf of Papua. Ranges from north Australia to New Guinea. Not common. Varies in colour from cream to dark brown; numerous fine axial ribs; two pairs of nodules, joined by a ridge between varices; spines short and often curved, and fewer in number than preceding species of similar form. Average length 75 mm.

10. **Haustellum haustellum** LINNE. New Britain, where it is reasonably common. Distributed throughout Indo-Pacific. Cream to fawn in colour, with irregular reddish-brown patches and spiral lines. Slightly nodulose between varices; aperture bright pink to orange; anterior canal long and without spines or scales. Average length 100 mm.

11. **Haustellum tweedianum** MACPHERSON. A common shell taken in prawn trawl nets on east coast of Australia. Similar in form to preceding species, but smaller, and with shorter anterior canal which is obsoletely spinose. Apex pink; aperture white. Average length 64 mm.

12. **Chicoreus ramosus** LINNE. Samarai, eastern Papua. Distribution — Indo-Pacific. Common. A large, showy shell attaining 300 mm in length, but shells from 150 to 200 mm make better cabinet specimens, as the larger ones are usually corroded, with imperfect varices. An unmistakable shell, with its glossy white aperture, and bright pink columella and lip.

13. **Chicoreus palma-rosae** LAMARCK. This scarce and lovely shell is very popular with collectors. Occurs from South-east Asia to north Australia, but is very rare in its southern range. Shell is cream to fawn, ornamented with numerous raised dark brown ribs. Fronds on varices are branched, and beautifully foliated, and often tipped with pink or lavender. Aperture white, with small denticles at edge of columella. Average length 90 mm.

PLATE 17
1
2
3
4
5
6
7
8
9
10
11
12
13

FAMILY MURICIDAE — continued.

1. **Chicoreus brunneus** LINK. Port Moresby. Distribution — Indo-Pacific. A common species. A dark brown shell with raised spiral bands and foliated varices dark brown to black; aperture white, columella and lip pink; one prominent knob between varices; columella smooth. Average length 65 mm.

2 and 3. **Chicoreus palmiferus** SOWERBY. North-west Australia, to which locality this species is restricted. Uncommon. Varies in colour from light orange-brown to dark brown; body whorl and aperture large; prominent raised gemmate spiral ribs of a darker colour; small denticles at columella edge, more prominent near anterior end. Average length 75 mm.

4. **Chicoreus torrefactus** SOWERBY. Port Moresby. Distribution — Indo-Pacific. Scarce in New Guinea waters. Figured specimen is an unusual colour form. Colour varies from light orange-brown to very dark brown. More elongate than previous species with which it is often confused. Body whorl with beaded spiral ribs and one to three knobs between varices. Aperture varies from cream to orange; columella smooth. Average length 70 mm.

5 to 7. **Euphyllon cornucervi** RÖDING. (=*E. monodon* SOWERBY.) Daru, western Papua. Distribution — north Australia and New Guinea. Uncommon. Another species that comes in many colours — white to blackish-brown. Fronds are long and curved; one prominent denticle on outer lip. Average length 75 mm.

8. **Chicoreus microphyllus** LAMARCK. Common on Papuan coast. Indo-Pacific distribution. A solid, elongate shell; coloured white, with numerous dark brown raised ribs; three nodules between varices; aperture white, edged with cream; columella with short plicae. Average length 75 mm.

9. **Hexaplex cichoreus** GMELIN. (=*H. endiva* LAMARK.) Manus Island, Admiralty Group. Distribution — Indo-Pacific. Scarce in New Guinea waters. A white shell ornamented with wide brown bands. Aperture white; columella smooth. Average length 65 mm.

10. **Chicoreus permaestus** HEDLEY. Yule Island, where it is abundant on intertidal mangrove roots. Western Pacific distribution. A dark burnt-brown shell with coarse spiral ribs; two to three low nodules between varices; aperture greyish-brown. Average length 50 mm.

11. **Euphyllon axicornis** LAMARCK. Dredged 22 metres. Port Moresby Harbour. Distribution — central Indo-Pacific and Indian Ocean. A scarce shell live collected. Fawn to light brown, fronds darker; two nodules between varices; aperture white; columella smooth. Average length 50 mm.

12. **Pterynotus triqueter** BORN. Rabaul, New Britain. Distribution — Indo-Pacific. A scarce shell that requires much cleaning to remove marine growth. Bluish-white with reddish-brown bands, the banding most conspicuous on the varices; aperture white. Average length 50 mm.

13. **Homalocantha scorpio** LINNE. New Ireland. Distributional range appears restricted to the central Indo-Pacific, and not common. When thoroughly cleaned the shell is light brown with dark brown to black fronded varices; five to six fronds on last whorl are splayed at extremities. Aperture bluish-grey. Average length 50 mm.

14. **Bassiella stainforthi** REEVE. Ranges from north-west Australia to Torres Strait. Uncommon. Numerous low fronded varices; white, with fronds dark brown to black; aperture pink. Average length 50 mm.

15. **Chicoreus denudatus** PERRY. Dredged off east coast of Australia. Reasonably common. Cream to fawn, with two nodules between varices tinted rusty-brown; varix with delicate short foliation; aperture white. Average length 40 mm.

16. **Chicoreus microphyllus** LAMARCK. A pale deepwater form dredged from 27 metres off Yule Island, Gulf of Papua. A fawn shell with six raised dark brown gemmate spiral bands, each with two to three low nodules between varices; edges of fronds faintly tinted with mauve; numerous short, barely visible denticles on outer edge of columella; outer lip dentate; aperture white; lip and edge of columella yellow. Figured specimen 44·45 mm.

17. **Pterochelus acanthopterus** LAMARCK. Intertidal to several metres depth from north and north-west Australia. Uncommon. Varying from cream to brown in colour, irregularly marked with longitudinal streaks of dark brown. Average length 65 mm.

PLATE 18
1
2
3
4
5
6
7
8
9
10
11
12
13
14
15
16
17

FAMILY MURICIDAE — continued.

1. **Pterynotus elongatus** SOLANDER. New Britain. Distribution — Indo-Pacific. A rare species. A long, narrow white shell; young specimens usually with some pink tints on varices and in aperture. Averages 65 mm.

2. **Pterynotus bipinnatus** REEVE. On intertidal reefs, Port Moresby. Distribution — central Indo-Pacific. Rare. Similar to preceding species, but smaller and narrower; varix less produced; anterior canal longer. Aperture is pinkish-mauve. Average length 40 mm.

3. **Homalocantha secunda** LAMARCK. North-west Australia. Range unknown. Rare. Usually with only last varix discernible; shell cream to light brown, fronds darker; prominent raised spiral ribs; five nodules on shoulder of whorl; aperture white; columella smooth. Figured specimen 38·1 mm.

4. **Homalocantha zamboi** BURCH & BURCH. On reef, shallow water, Siassi Islands, west New Britain. Appears to be restricted to the central Indo-Pacific and is moderately rare. Most attractive when properly cleaned. A bluish-white shell, bright pink about aperture. Possibly a variation of *H. anatomica* as some intergrading is evident. In this form, the extended digitations on old varices remain long and curved. Average length 50 mm.

5 and 6. Homalocantha pele PILSBRY. New Britain. Distribution — Indo-Pacific. Uncommon. Greyish-white, sometimes light pink about aperture, odd specimens yellow. Ornamented with two long extensions on varix at lip; old varices low and knobby. Average length 44 mm.

7 and 8. Pterynotus tripterus BORN. Dredged 22 metres west coast of Bougainville Island. Distribution, central Indo-Pacific. A scarce shell in fine live condition. Shell cream, with white flaring varices; aperture yellow; decorated with a longitudinal fold creating a single nodule between varices. Average length 40 mm.

9 and 10. Pterynotus alatus RÖDING. Dredged 37 metres off Yule Island, Papua. Distribution — central Indo-Pacific. Rare in choice live condition. A delicate white shell with coarse spiral ribs and one rounded nodule between varices; varices flared and crinkled. Average length 65 mm.

11. **Euphyllon cervicornis** LAMARCK. Dredged 25 metres, Gulf of Papua. Recorded from north Australia and New Guinea. Uncommon. A heavier shell than the normal form featured as Nos. 12 and 13. Other minor characters are evident that may warrant subspecific differentiation upon availability of more specimens for examination. This form is light brown in colour; strong spiral beaded ribs and longitudinal ridges creating three elongate nodules between varices; fronds unusually extended and branched like antlers; aperture and anterior canal tinted mauve. Average length 50 mm.

12 and 13. Euphyllon cervicornis LAMARCK. Dredged 55 metres off Oro Bay, north Papuan coast. Less robust than preceding form; a white, delicate shell, with fine branched antler-like fronds. Average length 40 mm.

14 and 15. Euphyllon damicornis HEDLEY. Taken in prawn trawl nets off Queensland coast. Uncommon. Shell cream to fawn; aperture flesh colour, sometimes yellow on outer lip and columella; prominent spiral ribs and two nodules between varices; upper fronds branched, lower ones foliated. Average length 40 mm.

16 and 17. Euphyllon longicornus DUNKER. (=*E. kurranulla* GARRARD; *recticornis* MARTENS.) Dredged from prawn grounds in south Queensland, to which locality it appears restricted. Shell cream to fawn; aperture white; spines long and only slightly curved, except for small ones on the rather long anterior canal; two nodules between varices. Average length 40 mm.

18. **Murexsul balteatus** SOWERBY. Rabaul, New Britain. Range not known. Appears scarce. A small white shell with six varices per whorl; fronds on varices coloured dark brown; aperture white. Average length 20 mm.

FAMILY COLUMBARIIDAE.

19. **Columbarium spinicinctum** VON MARTENS. (=*C. caragarang* GARRARD.) Trawled from deep water off Queensland coast. Appears restricted to this area where it is moderately rare. Distinguished by tall pagoda-like spire and long thin anterior canal. Shell fawn, with longitudinal streaks of brown; shoulder acutely angulate and sculptured with a row of numerous short flattened spines; a double row of scale-like projections below shoulder. Average length 75 mm.

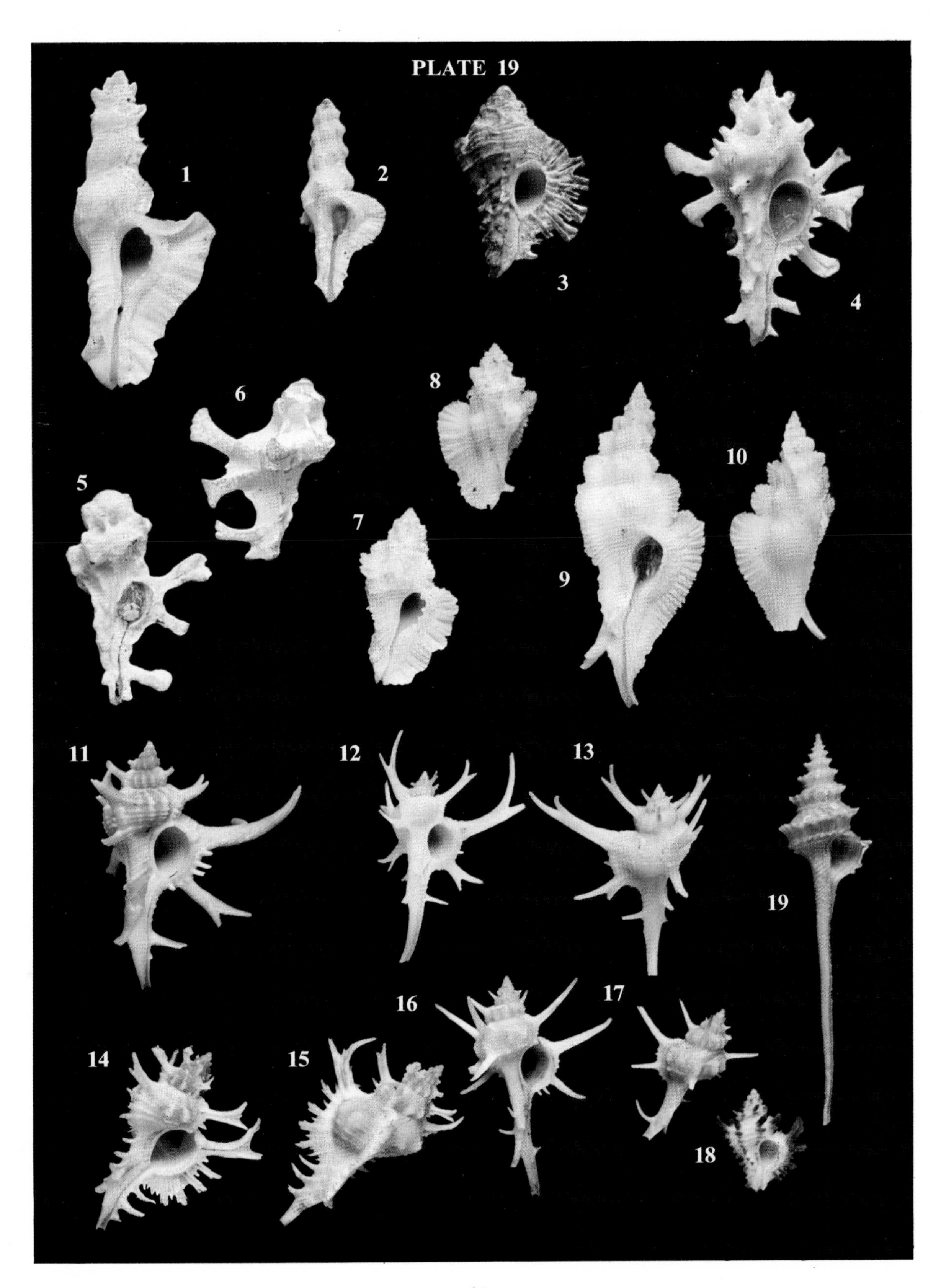
PLATE 19
1
2
3
4
5
6
7
8
9
10
11
12
13
14
15
16
17
18
19

FAMILY CORALLIOPHILIDAE (MAGILIDAE, RAPIDAE). A group of shells variable in form and sculpture, the common characteristic being an association with soft corals, on which they feed.

1. **Rapa rapa** LINNE. Port Moresby, embedded in soft sponge-like coral. Distribution — Indo-Pacific. Seldom found in live state because of unusual habitat. A thin shell, with large rounded body whorl; white to cream in colour, obscurely tinted with pink or mauve at anterior canal, and ornamented with spiral ribs that are more prominent near base. Average length 50 mm.

FAMILY MURICIDAE — SUBFAMILY THAISINAE includes the shells commonly known as oyster drills, drupes and purples.

2. **Vitularia miliaris** GMELIN. Siassi Islands, west New Britain. Indo-Pacific distribution. Uncommon. An orange coloured shell, with a granulose surface, and eight curving longitudinal ridges or varices which are marked alternately with dark brown and cream; aperture white; lip denticulate, with four blotches of orange and brown. Average length 45 mm.

3. **Rapana rapiformis** BORN. Dredged 15 metres off Sepik River, New Guinea. Distribution — Indo-Pacific. Reasonably common offshore. A light brown shell; inflated body whorl; large aperture; deep open umbilicus; fine spiral ribs; shoulder angulate with a row of hollow scale-like spines; suture channelled; aperture with fine white raised lines, and interstices dark brown. Average length 65 mm.

4 **Purpura persica** LINNE. Rabaul, New Britain. Distribution — Indo-Pacific. Reasonably common. Shell solid; large rounded body whorl and large aperture; dark brown in colour; fine spiral ribs and interrupted white lines; aperture white; outer lip dark brown; columella sometimes salmon-orange. Average length 65 mm.

5 and 6. **Nassa serta** BRUG. Intertidal reefs, Port Moresby. Distribution — Indo-Pacific. Reasonably common. Shell cream, tinted with pink, and irregularly banded and marked with brown; an ummarked spiral zone about centre of whorl; aperture cream to salmon. Averages 45 mm.

7. **Thais orbita** GMELIN. Intertidal on mid-Queensland coast. Ranges from Queensland to South Australia. Common. A solid shell; cream coloured; with prominent spaced spiral ribs. Average length 65 mm.

8. **Thais armigera** LINK. Trobriand Islands. Distribution — Indo-Pacific. Reasonably common. Fawn to light brown; three to four rows of nodules, most prominent at shoulder; aperture pink to flesh; outer lip denticulate, and marked with brown and yellow; columella is tinted salmon and yellow, and has three denticles anteriorly. Average length 65 mm.

9. **Thais tuberosa** RÖDING. Madang, New Guinea. Distribution — Indo-Pacific. Common. A solid shell; off-white in colour, marked with dark brown to black; nodulose spiral ridges, most prominent at shoulder; aperture cream, with reddish-brown lirae; columella with two salmon-brown blotches. Averages 45 mm.

10. **Thais luteostoma** HOLTEN. Port Moresby. Distribution — Indo-Pacific. Common. Spiral rows of nodules and fine raised ribs; brown in colour with axial lines of white between nodules; aperture white, marked with cream to orange; outer lip dark brown. Average length 40 mm.

11. **Mancinella alouina** RÖDING. Yule Island, Papua. Distribution — Indo-Pacific. Common. A cream shell with numerous sharp nodules of reddish-brown, and some fine spiral lines of similar colour; aperture orange and lirate. Average length 40 mm.

12. **Drupella cornus** RÖDING. Yule Island, Papua. Distribution — Indo-Pacific. Not common. A solid shell; white; four rows of spinous nodules; aperture white; three rounded teeth on inside of outer lip; two to three plicae on lower part of columella. Average length 32 mm.

13. **Thais aculeata** DESHAYES AND MILNE-EDWARDS. Port Moresby. Distribution — Indo-Pacific. Common. Greyish-brown; five rows of nodules, coloured white between nodules; aperture white blotched with purplish-brown; outer lip has five denticles and columella three low plicate ridges. Average length 40 mm.

14. **Thais intermedia** KIENER. Yule Island, Papua. Distribution — Indo-Pacific. Common. Similar to preceding species, nodules fewer, lower and less spinous; aperture with more numerous and smaller denticles. Average length 32 mm.

15. **Drupina grossularia** RÖDING. Abundant on intertidal reefs throughout New Guinea. Distribution — Indo-Pacific. Common. Fawn coloured, usually heavily encrusted with coral growth; low spired; rows of nodules; two prominent projections at lip, uppermost one open; aperture orange-yellow; outer lip with six white denticles. Average length 32 mm.

16. **Drupa morum** RÖDING. Port Moresby. Distribution — Indo-Pacific. Common. An attractive species when properly cleaned. White, with dark brown nodules; aperture deep lavender, with prominent groups of denticles; columella with three strong plicate ridges. Average 32 mm.

17. **Drupa rubusidaea** RÖDING. Siassi Islands, western New Britain. Distribution — Indo-Pacific. Uncommon. A fawn shell with numerous scale-like spinous nodules and gemmate spiral ribs; aperture cream to yellow; columella pinkish-lavender; denticles on lip and plicate ridges on columella, more numerous and lower than in previous species. Average length 32 mm.

18. **Drupa ricina** LINNE. Port Moresby. Distribution — Indo-Pacific. Common. A white shell, with four to five rows of black-tipped spinous nodules; narrow aperture, which is white edged with squarish patches of orange and with prominent grouped denticles; columella plicate. Average length 25 mm.

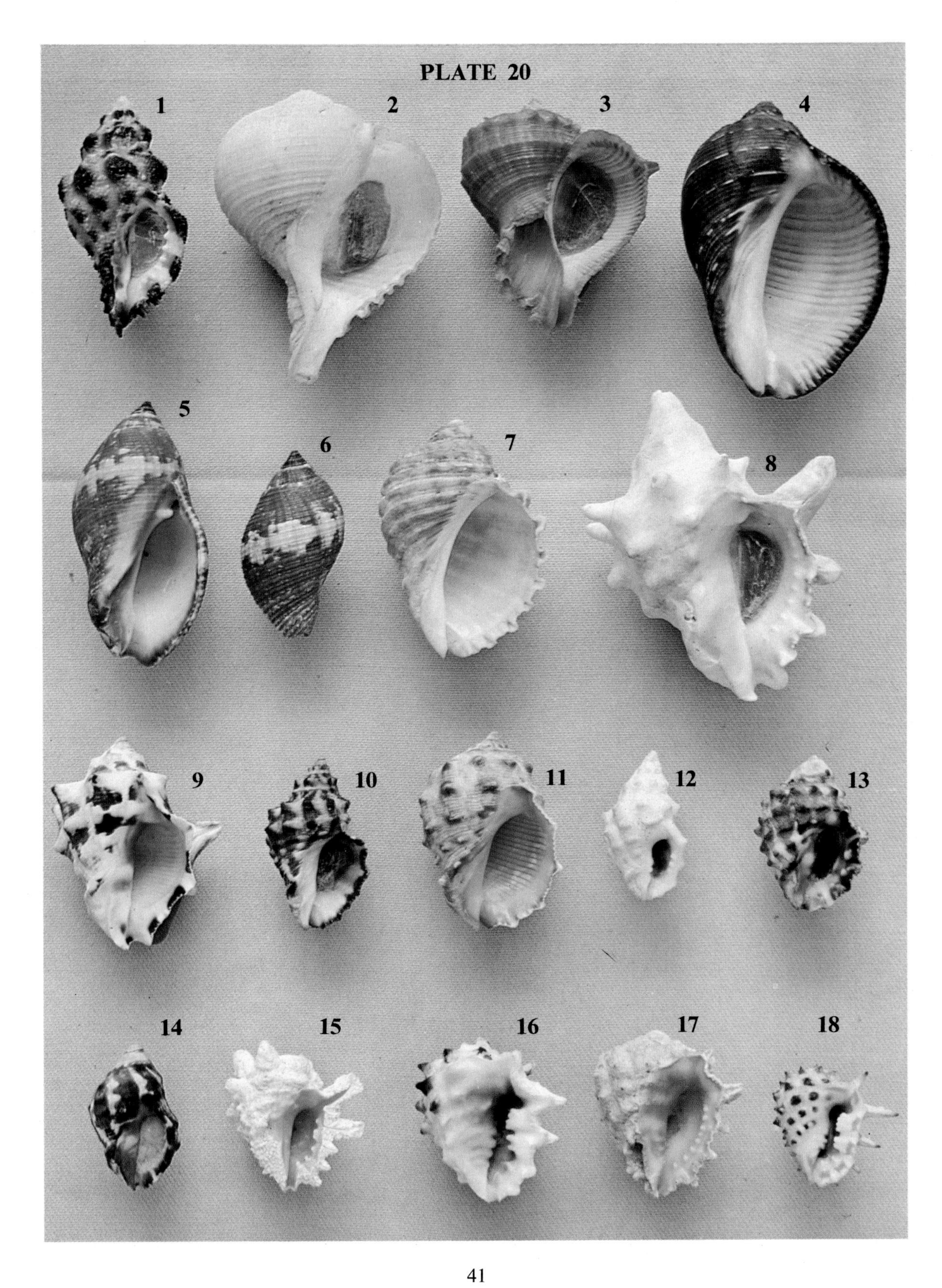
PLATE 20
1
2
3
4
5
6
7
8
9
10
11
12
13
14
15
16
17
18

FAMILY VASIDAE. A small group of heavy shells that are mostly nodulose, and sometimes spinous. The aperture is toothed, and the operculum is horny and sickle shaped.

1. **Tudicula rasilistoma** ABBOTT. Dredged 128 metres, Queensland. Ranges from Queensland to New South Wales. Uncommon. A solid shell, with six to eight rounded knobs on shoulder, and prominent axial growth lines. Cream, with longitudinal streaks of dark brown. Aperture cream, tinted with pink; juvenile specimens more vividly coloured. Three low teeth on columella. Average length 75 mm.
2. **Vasum ceramicum** LINNE. Port Moresby. Distribution — Indo-Pacific. Common. A heavy, coarsely sculptured shell, with a row of produced nodules at shoulder. Dark brown, with narrow bands of white. Aperture white; three teeth on columella. Average length 90 mm.
3. **Vasum turbinellum** LINNE. Yule Island, Papua. Distribution — Indo-Pacific. Common. Smaller than preceding species, and with less produced spire. Average length 50 mm.
4. **Tudicula armigera** A. ADAMS. Taken in prawn trawl nets off Queensland coast. A scarce shell. Has a long anterior canal, and long spines on shoulder and base of shell. Cream coloured with broken bands of reddish-brown. Aperture white to cream; some specimens pinkish. Average length 50 mm.

FAMILY HARPIDAE. Another group with only a few members, but includes some well-known shells because of their exquisite sculpture and intricate blending of colour pattern. The harp shells have large body whorls, and large, open apertures; old varices form raised longitudinal ridges; an enamelled callus covers the columella; they have no teeth in aperture; and lack an operculum.

5. **Harpa amouretta** RÖDING. Port Moresby. Distribution — Indo-Pacific. Common. A small elongate species, with relatively tall spire. Longitudinal ribs are crossed by fine light and dark brown lines, and are highly polished. Interstices with dull finish, and marked with wavy patterns of purplish-brown, light brown and cream. Average length 45 mm.
6. **Harpa articularis** LAMARCK. Manus Island, Admiralty Group. Distribution appears restricted to central Indo-Pacific, and rather scarce. Body whorl is less inflated, and spire more produced, than in following species. Longitudinal ribs crossed by black and white bands. A purplish-brown blotch covers most of ventral surface. Average length 60 mm.
7. **Harpa major** RÖDING. Samarai, eastern Papua. Distribution — Indo-Pacific. Reasonably common. A large shell, with inflated body whorl. Ribs with broad, pale bands, and columella with two nut-brown blotches. Averages 90 mm.
8. **Harpa major** RÖDING. Dorsal view.
9. **Harpa davidis** RÖDING. Dredged 9 metres near Samarai, eastern Papua. Distribution — Indo-Pacific. Common. Similar to previous species, ribs narrower and more definitely banded. Base with single large dark-brown blotch. Average length 75 mm.
10. **Harpa harpa** LINNE. Trobriand Islands. Distribution — central Indo-Pacific. Uncommon over most of its range, but reasonably abundant in the New Guinea islands. A medium sized shell, probably the most beautiful of the harps. Ribs crossed by fine black lines; interstices ornamented with wavy lines of many colours, and usually with a row of large squarish red blotches about centre of body whorl. Entire surface highly polished. Columella with three purplish-brown blotches. Averages 60 mm.
11. **Harpa harpa** LINNE. Ventral view.

The **FAMILY MITRIDAE** is a large family of shells, and most species are abundant, particularly in the tropical seas, where they occur in colonies on shallow patches of sand and on intertidal coral reefs. Collecting at night, with lights, is most rewarding, as the snails leave a trail in the sandy bottom. The mitres vary in size from less than 12 mm to the heavy 150 mm shells of *M. mitra* LINNE. They are extremely variable in form and colour, some species being most attractive. Most have a tall, tapering spire, and several strong columella folds or teeth.

12. **Nebularia cardinalis** GMELIN. Samarai, Papua. Distribution — Indo-Pacific. Common. A white shell, with fine punctate spiral grooves and rows of irregularly shaped reddish-brown spots and blotches. Aperture white, with five teeth. Average length 60 mm.
13. **Chrysame eremitarum** RÖDING. Port Moresby. Common throughout Indo-Pacific. Cream to fawn, with axial streaks and blotches of dark brown. Fine spiral grooves; aperture cream; columella with five teeth. Average length 65 mm.
14. **Chrysame eremiatrum** RÖDING. Dorsal view.
15. **Mitra mitra** LINNE. Trobriand Islands. Distribution — Indo-Pacific. Common. A large, heavy shell attaining 150 mm and more. White and smooth, ornamented with spiral rows of squarish blotches of red, and one row of larger, irregular red blotches below sutures. Average length 115 mm.
16. **Mitra mitra** LINNE. Ventral view.
17. **Mitra papalis** LINNE. New Britain. Distribution — Indo-Pacific. Uncommon. A white shell, ornamented with numerous rows of small and medium sized spots and blotches of reddish-brown. Body whorl nearly smooth, crimped at sutures. Aperture cream, with six teeth. Average length 100 mm.

PLATE 21
1
2
3
4
5
6
7
8
9
10
11
12
13
14
15
16
17

FAMILY MITRIDAE — continued

1. Chrysame ferruginea LAMARCK. New Britain. Indo-Pacific range. Common. Cream with squarish rusty-brown blotches; strong spiral ribs. Average length 45 mm.

2. Chrysame imperialis RÖDING. New Britain. Indo-Pacific range. Uncommon. Burnt orange colour, with patches of white and brown. Punctate grooves and coronated at suture. Average length 50 mm.

3. Mitra stictica LINK. Samarai, Papua. Indo-Pacific range. Common. White with rows of reddish blotches; strongly coronated at sutures. Averages 50 mm.

4. Chrysame nigra GMELIN. Papua. Range — Pacific Ocean. Uncommon. Relatively smooth; dark brown, with minute white spots at suture. Average length 50 mm.

5 and 6. Pterygia nucea GMELIN. New Britain. Indo-Pacific range. Uncommon. Colour variable as indicated by illustrations. Averages 40 mm.

7 and 8. Strigatella scutulata GMELIN. Port Moresby. Indo-Pacific range. Common. Dark brown with white axial streaks, varying in density. Averages 25 mm.

9. Neocancilla granatina LAMARCK. New Britain. Indo-Pacific range. Uncommon. White, with two bands of reddish-brown, and fine interrupted lines; granulated spiral ridges. Average length 45 mm.

10. Pterygia dactylus LINNE. Port Moresby. Indo-Pacific range. Uncommon. White, with three to five interrupted bands of brown, and some thin lines. Average 40 mm.

11. Swainsonia casta GMELIN. New Britain. Indo-Pacific range. Common. Smooth shell; white, with broad brown band. Average length 45 mm.

12. Chrysame ambigua SWAINSON. Papua. Indo-Pacific range. Common. Dark brown with lighter band below suture; spiral grooves. Average length 50 mm.

13. Pterygia fenestrata LAMARCK. Bougainville Island. Indo-Pacific range. Reasonably common. Low spire; long aperture; white, with narrow dark brown bands on raised surface between grooves. Average length 25 mm.

14. Neocancilla scabricula LINNE. West New Britain. Indo-Pacific range. Scarce. White with brown and white spots on strong spiral cords; some reddish-brown blotching. Average length 30 mm.

15. Neocancilla papilio LINK. Port Moresby. Indo-Pacific range. Common. White, with black spots on strong spiral ribs, and two brown bands. Averages 40 mm.

16. Pterygia crenulata GMELIN. Papua. Indo-Pacific range. Uncommon. White, densely but irregularly marked with light brown; sculptured with low spiral cords. Averages 25 mm.

17. Neocancilla clathrus GMELIN. Port Moresby. Indo-Pacific range. Reasonably common. Colour pinkish, with two bands of dark brown blotches; spiral cords and axial grooves. Average length 25 mm.

18. Chrysame tornata REEVE. New Britain. Pacific Ocean range. Scarce. Golden-brown; sculptured with prominent spiral ribs. Average length 25 mm.

19. Chrysame cucumerina LAMARCK. Port Moresby. Indo-Pacific range. Common. Small and solid; with strong spiral ribs; reddish-brown, with wide interrupted white band. Averages 20 mm.

20. Chrysame coronata LAMARCK. New Britain. Pacific Ocean range. Uncommon. Dark brown; white coronations below suture; spiral cords. Average length 20 mm.

21. Imbricaria conus GMELIN. New Britain. Indo-Pacific range. Uncommon. This and following species resemble cone shells. Grey-brown; thin reddish spiral lines; punctate grooves; prominent white coronations at shoulder. Average length 25 mm.

22. Imbricaria conularis LAMARCK. Port Moresby. Indo-Pacific range. Common. Comparatively smooth; ash-grey, with rows of fine brown lines, and oddly shaped white blotches. Average 20 mm.

23. Cancilla peasei DOHRN. Off-shore, Papua. Pacific Ocean range. Uncommon. White, with elevated ribs lined with reddish-brown. Average length 30 mm.

24. Cancilla praestantissima RÖDING. Port Moresby Harbour, 18 metres. Indo-Pacific range. Uncommon. Slender; cream to fawn, with reddish-brown spiral ribs. Average length 30 mm.

25. Cancilla circula KIENER. New Britain. Indo-Pacific range. Scarce. Rich honey-brown colour; yellow band below suture; elevated ribs coloured burnt-orange. Average length 30 mm.

26. Cancilla interlirata REEVE. Off-shore, Port Moresby. Indo-Pacific range. Seldom collected alive. Broad and narrow cords; colour variable. Average length 30 mm.

27. Cancilla filaris LINNE. New Britain. Indo-Pacific range. Common. Spire shorter than preceding species; creamy-white with reddish elevated ribs. Average length 25 mm.

28. Cancilla verrucosa REEVE. New Britain. Pacific Ocean range. Uncommon. Cream to grey with brown band, and brown dashes between spinous nodules. Average length 20 mm.

29. Strigatella aurantia GMELIN. Port Moresby. Pacific Ocean range. Common. Dark brown with an orange band below suture; deep spiral grooves. Average length 25 mm.

30. Swainsonia desetangsii KIENER. New Britain. Western Pacific range. Uncommon. Cream, with irregular squarish brown blotches and row of brown spots below suture; deep spiral grooves. 25 mm.

31. Strigatella auriculoides REEVE. Samarai, Papua. Indo-Pacific range. Uncommon. Dark brown with an interrupted cream band; fine spiral grooves. Average length 20 mm.

32. Nebularia doliolum KUSTER. West New Britain. Indo-Pacific range. Uncommon. Burnt-orange colour; deep grooves of brown. Averages 20 mm.

33. Chrysame contracta SWAINSON. New Britain. Indo-Pacific range. Scarce species. White, with two bands of brown blotches. Average length 30 mm.

34. Dibaphus edentulus SWAINSON. Samarai, Papua. Indo-Pacific range. Scarce. Lacks teeth or columella folds; outer lip thickened. Creamy-yellow with two bands of longitudinal brown streaks; fine spiral grooves. Superficially resembles *Conus mitratus*. Average 20 mm.

35. Strigatella acuminata SWAINSON. Port Moresby. Indo-Pacific range. Common. Coloured yellow; smooth body whorl; tall sharp spire. Average length 25 mm.

36. Strigatella litterata LAMARCK. Port Moresby. Indo-Pacific range. Common. White, with two bands of brown figurations, and fine punctate spiral grooves. Average length 25 mm.

37. Strigatella retusa LAMARCK. New Britain. Indo-Pacific range. Common. Dark brown with axial lines of creamy-white, and narrow white spiral band. Average length 20 mm.

38. Nebularia fraga QUOY & GAIMARD. Port Moresby. Indo-Pacific range. Common. Dark brown, with yellow dashes on elevated ribs. Average length 20 mm.

39. Strigatella oleacea REEVE. West New Britain. Indo-Pacific range. Reasonably common. Smooth; brown, with white aperture. 20 mm.

40 and 41. Cancilla bacillum LAMARCK. Port Moresby. Pacific Ocean range. Common. Blue-grey with green or brown axial streaks; deep spiral grooves. Average length 25 mm.

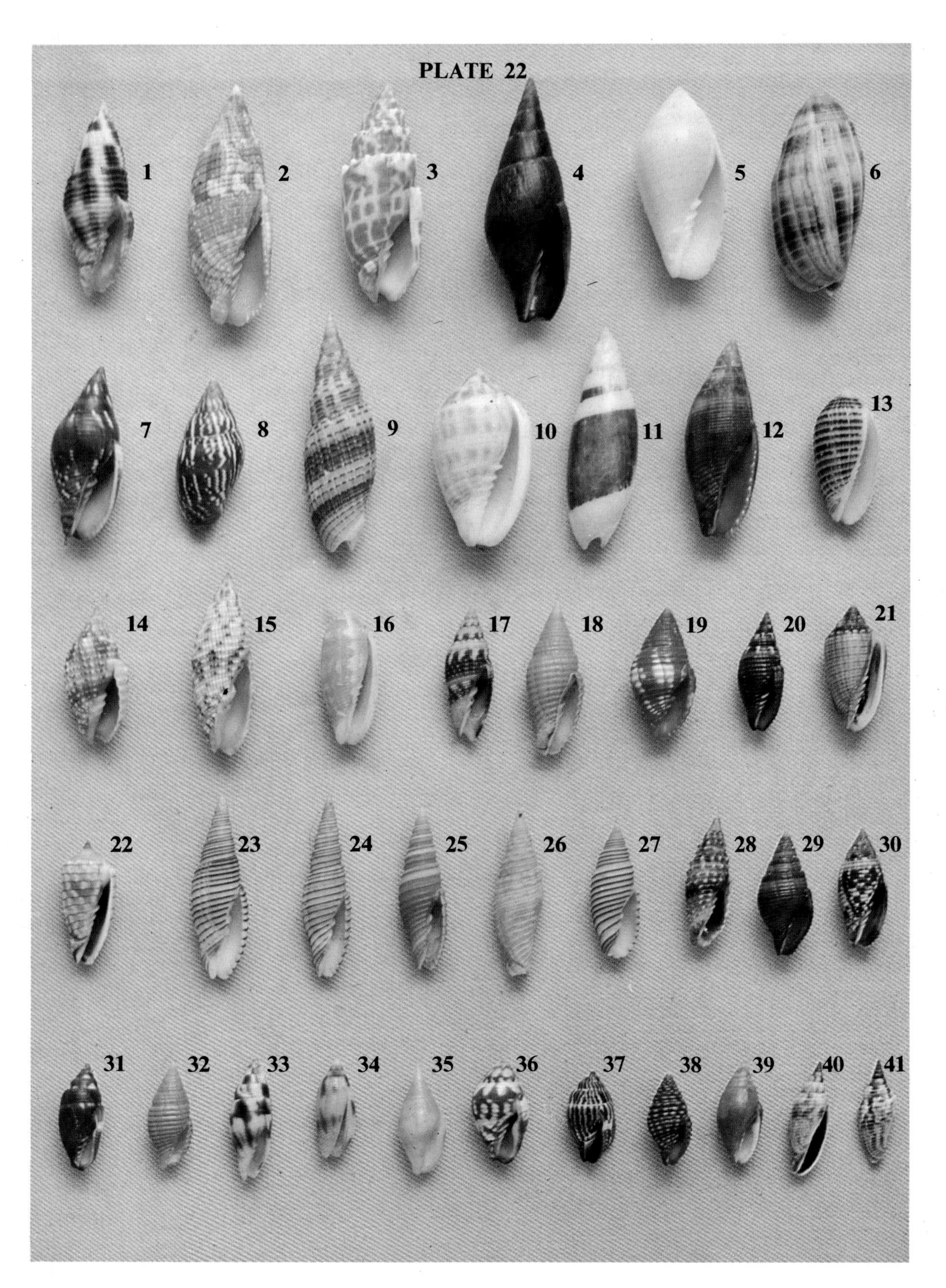
PLATE 22
1
2
3
4
5
6
7
8
9
10
11
12
13
14
15
16
17
18
19
20
21
22
23
24
25
26
27
28
29
30
31
32
33
34
35
36
37
38
39
40
41

FAMILY MITRIDAE — continued.

1. Nebularia tabanula LAMARCK. New Britain. Indo-Pacific range. Uncommon. Small brown shell with strong spiral ribs. Average length 12 mm.

2 and 3. Strigatella telescopium REEVE. Misima Island, Papua. Pacific range. Scarce. Comparatively smooth; brown, with cream band below suture. Average length 20 mm.

4. Nebularia amaura HERVIER. Misima Island, Papua. Pacific range. Rare. Brown, with narrow yellow band below suture; spiral grooves and axial ribs. Average length 20 mm.

5. Imbricaria olivaeformis SWAINSON. New Britain. Pacific range. Common. As name suggests, this species resembles an olive shell. Smooth; yellow; apex and base purple. To 20 mm.

6. Imbricaria punctata SWAINSON. Port Moresby. Indo-Pacific range. Common. Cream, with punctate spiral grooves. To 14 mm.

7. Imbricaria vanikorensis QOUY & GAIMARD. New Britain. Pacific range. Uncommon. Cream, with row of white spots below suture, and some white spotting on whorl. Average length 20 mm.

8. Subcancilla malleti PETIT DE LA SAUSSAYE. 50 metres, Gulf of Papua. Rare. Prominent spiral ridges and axial ribs; shell, brown, with obsolete white axial streaks. Average length 12 mm.

9. Mitra peculiaris REEVE. New Britain. Pacific range. Rare. Cream, with brown band and thin dark line at suture; keeled shoulder etched with white. Average length 12 mm.

FAMILY TEREBRIDAE. Most of the larger auger shells from shallow water are brightly coloured, whilst their relatives from deeper water are often intricately sculptured. They are a large family, and popular with collectors. The terebras are carnivores, and possess a brown, horny operculum.

10. Hastula albula MENKE. Port Moresby. Indo-Pacific range. Common. Cream, with white band below suture; some brown axial streaks; smooth except for axial folds below sutures. Average length 25 mm.

11 and 12. Hastula strigilata LINNE. Colour variations from Yule Island, Papua. Pacific range. Common. Fawn to grey, with a row of dark spots on white band below suture; axial ribs. Average length 25 mm.

13. Terebra nitida HINDS. New Britain. Indo-Pacific range. Uncommon. Uniformly brown; axial ribs; row of punctures below sutures. Average length 20 mm.

14. Terebra multistriata SCHEPMAN. 40 metres, Gulf of Papua. Indo-Pacific range. Rare. Cream, with brown band; strong axial ribs and fine spiral grooves. Average length 25 mm.

15. Terebra turrita E. A. SMITH. Dredged, Gulf of Papua. Pacific range. Rare. Similar to preceding species, but has row of punctures below suture. Average length 25 mm.

16. Terebra laevigata GRAY. Port Moresby. Indo-Pacific range. Uncommon. Fawn; whitish raised cord at suture; fine spiral grooves. Average length 40 mm.

17. Terebra funiculata HINDS. Bougainville Island. Pacific range. Scarce. Creamy-white, with spiral grooves of reddish-brown. Average length 30 mm.

18. Terebra longiscata DESHAYES. Yule Island, Papua. Pacific range. Uncommon. Colour variable, figured specimen brown. Strong axial ribs; fine spiral grooves; deep punctate groove below suture. Average length 30 mm.

19. Terebra kilburni BURCH. Port Moresby. Range, New Guinea to Fiji. Uncommon. Creamy-yellow with raised white beads at suture, and strong whitish axial ribs. Average 25 mm.

20. Terebra paucistriata E. A. SMITH. New Britain. Range, New Guinea to Fiji. Scarce. Fawn, with two rows of white beads at suture; strong axial ribs, with brown interstices longitudinally punctate. Average length 25 mm.

21. Terebra amanda HINDS. New Britain. Indo-Pacific range. Uncommon. Orange-brown, with row of white beads at suture, and several rows of fine punctate grooves. Average 40 mm.

22. Terebra columellaris HINDS. Port Moresby. Pacific range. Common. White with large orange blotches, and a row of white beads at suture; rounded and curved axial ribs; spiral groove in interstices. Average length 40 mm.

23. Terebra undulata GRAY. Port Moresby. Pacific range. Common. Orange-brown, with a row of white beads at suture, and longitudinal brown lines in interstices of the prominent axial ribs. Average length 40 mm.

24. Terebra affinis GRAY. Port Moresby. Indo-Pacific range. Common. Off-white, with a row of squarish brown blotches on body whorl; low axial ribs; fine spiral grooves. Average length 40 mm.

25. Hastula stylata HINDS. New Britain. Pacific range. Scarce. Olive-brown, with white and brown bands, often overlapping below sutures; longitudinal folds at sutures. Average length 30 mm.

26. Terebra succincta GMELIN. Port Moresby. Pacific range. Uncommon. Uniformly dark brown; handsome sculpturing of fine curving axial ribs and numerous spiral ridges; a deep groove below suture forming a row of raised beads. Average length 40 mm.

27. Terebra conspersa HINDS. Port Moresby. Range, New Guinea to Fiji. Uncommon. Whorls flattened; cream to greyish, with irregular brown spots at sutures and odd brown blotches; fine axial and spiral ridges; and low sutural band. Average length 40 mm.

28. Terebra species. Possibly a variation of *T. fenestrata* HINDS. Dredged 30 metres, Gulf of Papua. Cream with reddish-brown streaks; axial ribs and spiral ridges forming a granulose pattern; one strong and a second weaker row of beads at suture. Figured specimen 45 mm.

29. Terebra myuros LAMARCK. Dredged, Port Moresby Harbour. Pacific range. Rare. White, with clearly defined but irregularly shaped reddish-brown blotches. Two rows of beads at suture, and fine spiral ridges. Average length 55 mm.

30. Terebra cingulifera LAMARCK. Port Moresby. Indo-Pacific range. Common. Honey-brown in colour; prominent sutural ridge; fine spiral grooves and axial growth lines. Average length 65 mm.

31. Terebra fenestrata HINDS. Dredged, Gulf of Papua. Pacific range. Scarce. Cream, with some light to reddish-brown zones; two rows of beads; axial ribs and spiral ridges. Average length 50 mm.

32. Terebra straminia GRAY. Samarai, Papua. Pacific range. Scarce. A brown shell, with a row of longitudinally-elongate beads; axial ribs and spiral ridges. Average length 50 mm.

33. Terebra jenningsi BURCH. Port Moresby. Pacific range. Uncommon. Creamy-yellow, with raised white band at suture, otherwise comparatively smooth. Averages 50 mm.

34. Terebra triseriata GRAY. Dredged 37 metres, Gulf of Papua. Pacific range. Uncommon. A long slender shell of many whorls. Cream to light brown; sculptured with two to three rows of beads at suture, and spiral cords between sutures. Average length 75 mm.

35 and 36. Hastula lanceata LINNE. Port Moresby. Indo-Pacific range. Uncommon. A smooth shell with some axial folds on early whorls. Colour variable, but unmistakeably marked with wavy longitudinal brown lines. Average length 45 mm.

37. Impages hectica LINNE. Trobriand Islands, eastern Papua. Indo-Pacific range. Reasonably common. Smooth, usually creamy-white, variably blotched and spotted with dark brown. Odd specimens are nearly black, others white. Average length 50 mm.

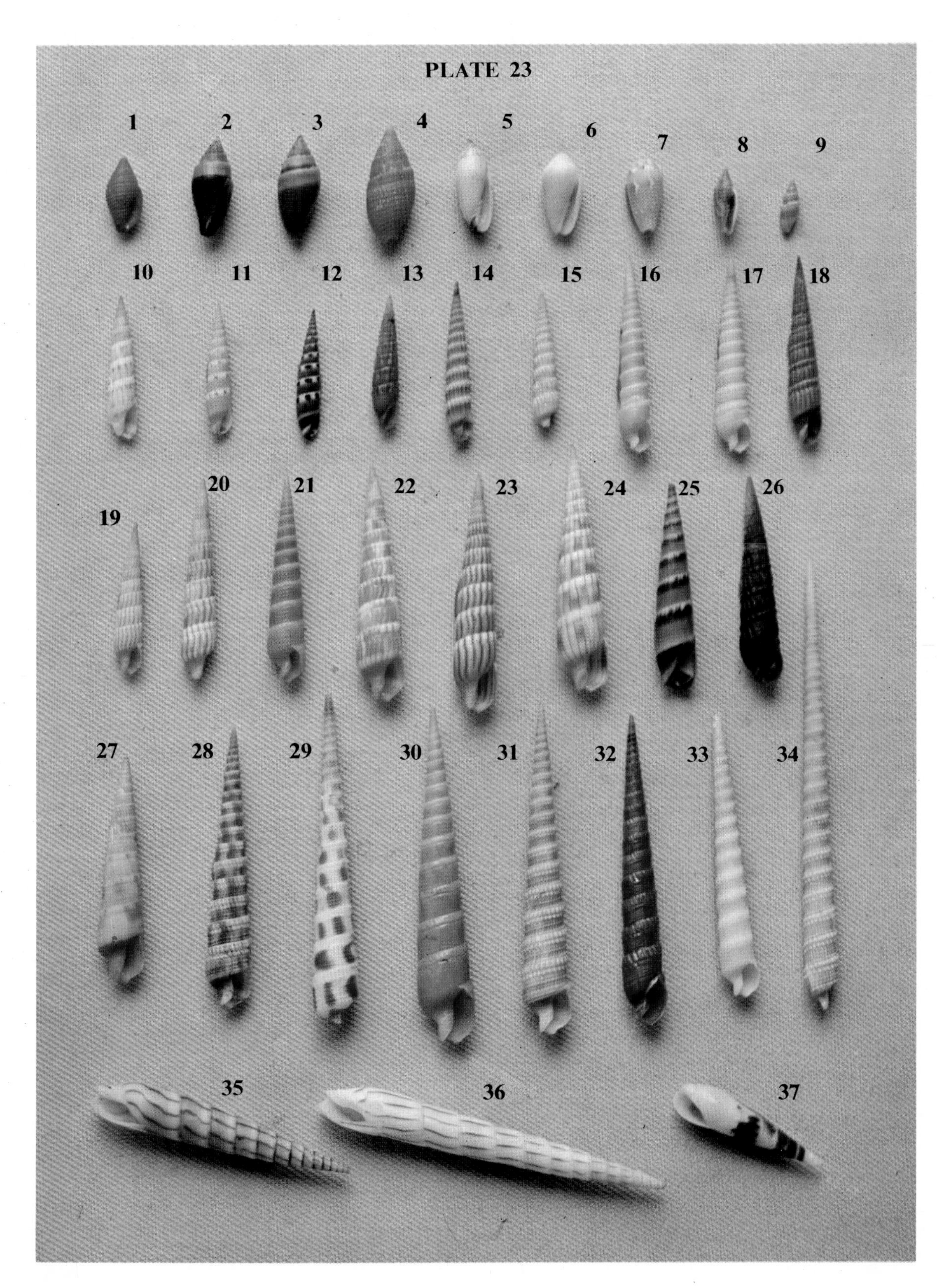
PLATE 23
1
2
3
4
5
6
7
8
9
10
11
12
13
14
15
16
17
18
19
20
21
22
23
24
25
26
27
28
29
30
31
32
33
34
35
36
37

FAMILY TEREBRIDAE — continued.

1. **Terebra crenulata** LINNE. Port Moresby. Indo-Pacific range. Common. This typical form is fawn coloured, with two rows of fine brown spots, and is crenulated at sutures. Average length 100 mm.

2. **Terebra crenulata** LINNE (forma *fimbriata* DESHAYES.) Lacks the strong crenulations of the typical form, and is uncommon.

3. **Terebra crenulata** LINNE. Port Moresby. An unusual colour variation which was collected with No. 8 (figured below), indicating the possibility of interbreeding when these species share the same habitat.

4. **Terebra maculata** LINNE. Port Moresby. Indo-Pacific range. Common. The largest of the auger shells, averaging 180 mm, but odd specimens much larger. Smooth; creamy-white, with four to five broken bands of light brown and two rows of blotches below suture.

5. **Terebra dimidiata** LINNE. New Britain. Indo-Pacific range. Reasonably common. Comparatively smooth, orange in colour, with irregular creamy-white axial streaks. Average length 100 mm.

6. **Terebra guttata** RÖDING. Port Moresby. Indo-Pacific range. Uncommon. Comparatively smooth, orange-brown, with two rows of large, slightly raised, white spots, one row below suture and the other at base of body whorl. Average length 100 mm.

7. **Terebra areolata** LINK. (=*T. muscaria* LAMARK.) Port Moresby. Indo-Pacific range. Common. Smooth; cream coloured, with three rows of dark brown squarish spots on pre-whorls, and four rows on body whorl. Averages 115 mm.

8. **Terebra areolata** LINK. An unusual colour form. See comments for No. 3 above.

9. **Terebra subulata** LINNE. Samarai, eastern Papua. Indo-Pacific range. Common. Similar to preceding species, but easily distinguished by its more slender form, and one row less of brown spots, having two rows on pre-whorls, and three on body whorl. Average length 125 mm.

10. **Terebra duplicata** LINNE. Yule Island, Gulf of Papua. Range — north Australia to New Guinea. Uncommon. Uniformly dark brown, with a deep groove below suture, and deep curving longitudinal grooves. Average length 75 mm.

11. **Terebra chlorata** LAMARCK. Port Moresby. Indo-Pacific range. Common. A smooth shell; white, with brown or mauve blotches and axial streaks; spiral groove at suture. Average length 55 mm.

12. **Terebra felina** DILLWYN. Port Moresby. Indo-Pacific range. Reasonably common. Comparatively smooth; a groove below sutures; white, with a row of small reddish-brown spots, sometimes merging, at centre of body whorl. Average length 65 mm.

13. **Terebra albomarginata** DESHAYES. 35 metres, Gulf of Papua. Range — north-east Australia to New Guinea. Scarce in good condition. Orange-brown, with a white sutural band. Several punctate spiral grooves and curved axial growth lines. Average length 75 mm.

14. **Terebra argus** HINDS. Port Moresby. Pacific range. Uncommon. Comparatively smooth, with faint axial growth lines. Cream coloured, with three to four bands of pale fawn, squarish spots. Average length 65 mm.

15. **Terebra cerithina** LAMARCK. Yule Island, Papua. Indo-Pacific range. Common. Cream to light blue-grey, with irregular light brown axial lines and spiral bands. Punctate groove near suture forming a low beaded band; numerous flat axial ribs. Average length 50 mm.

16. **Terebra nebulosa** SOWERBY. Port Moresby. Indo-Pacific range. Reasonably common. Creamy-white, with dense nebulose reddish-brown patches; punctate groove below suture forming a low white beaded band; prominent axial ribs, with grooves in interstices. Average length 50 mm.

17. **Terebra babylonia** LAMARCK. Port Moresby. Indo-Pacific range. Common. Creamy-white, with reddish-brown shallow axial grooves; spiral groove at suture forming a low beaded band. Average length 50 mm.

18. **Terebra pertusa** BORN. New Britain. Pacific range. Scarce species. Whorls flattened; light brown in colour, with a sutural band of alternating dark brown and cream axial ridges; curved longitudinal ribs, and punctate spiral grooves. Average length 55 mm.

19. **Terebra pallida** DESHAYES. 30 metres, Gulf of Papua. Pacific Ocean range. Scarce. A uniform tan colour; low sutural band; axial folds at the sutures, and spiral grooves. Averages 65 mm.

20 and 21. **Terebra anilis** RÖDING. 35 metres, Gulf of Papua. Pacific range. Uncommon. Variable in colour from cream to dark brown; two rows of angled beadings at suture; numerous axial ribs crossed by spiral grooves. Averages 65 mm.

FAMILY VEXILLIDAE. Until recently, the genera *Vexillum* and *Pusia* have been placed with the Mitridae, but recent studies of the animals suggest sufficient disparity to warrant separation. Members of this group have prominent axial ribs, often nodulose at the shoulders, and most species are brilliantly marked or attractively sculptured.

22, 23 and 24. **Vexillum vulpeculum** LINNE. Port Moresby. Pacific range. Common. Colourful but extremely variable. Usually a bright orange, with one to several bands of dark brown; prominent axial fold-like ribs, and fine spiral grooves. Average length 50 mm.

25 and 26. **Vexillum taeniatum** LAMARCK. Port Moresby. Indo-Pacific range. Only moderately rare, but the vivid colour pattern appeals to collectors, and it always commands a high price on dealers' lists. Sculpture consists of fine, even axial ribs, and spiral grooves. Anterior canal much recurved. Average length 50 mm.

27. **Vexillum subdivisum** GMELIN. Yule Island, Papua, Indo-Pacific range. Uncommon. A slender shell; greyish, with narrow dark brown bands; numerous narrow but prominent axial ribs, with grooves in interstices. Average length 40 mm.

28. **Vexillum rugosum** GMELIN. Port Moresby. Indo-Pacific range. Common. Grey to light brown with two to three dark brown bands; strong axial ribs, nodulose at shoulder; deep spiral grooves. Average length 30 mm.

29. **Vexillum caffrum** LINNE. Yule Island, Papua. Indo-Pacific range. Reasonably common. Dark brown with one or two narrow yellow-orange bands; body whorl comparatively smooth; early whorls axially ribbed. Average length 45 mm.

30. **Vexillum plicarium** LINNE. Port Moresby. Indo-Pacific range. Common. Off-white to light grey; one broad dark brown band, and two interrupted narrow bands; prominent axial ribs and fine spiral grooves. Average length 45 mm.

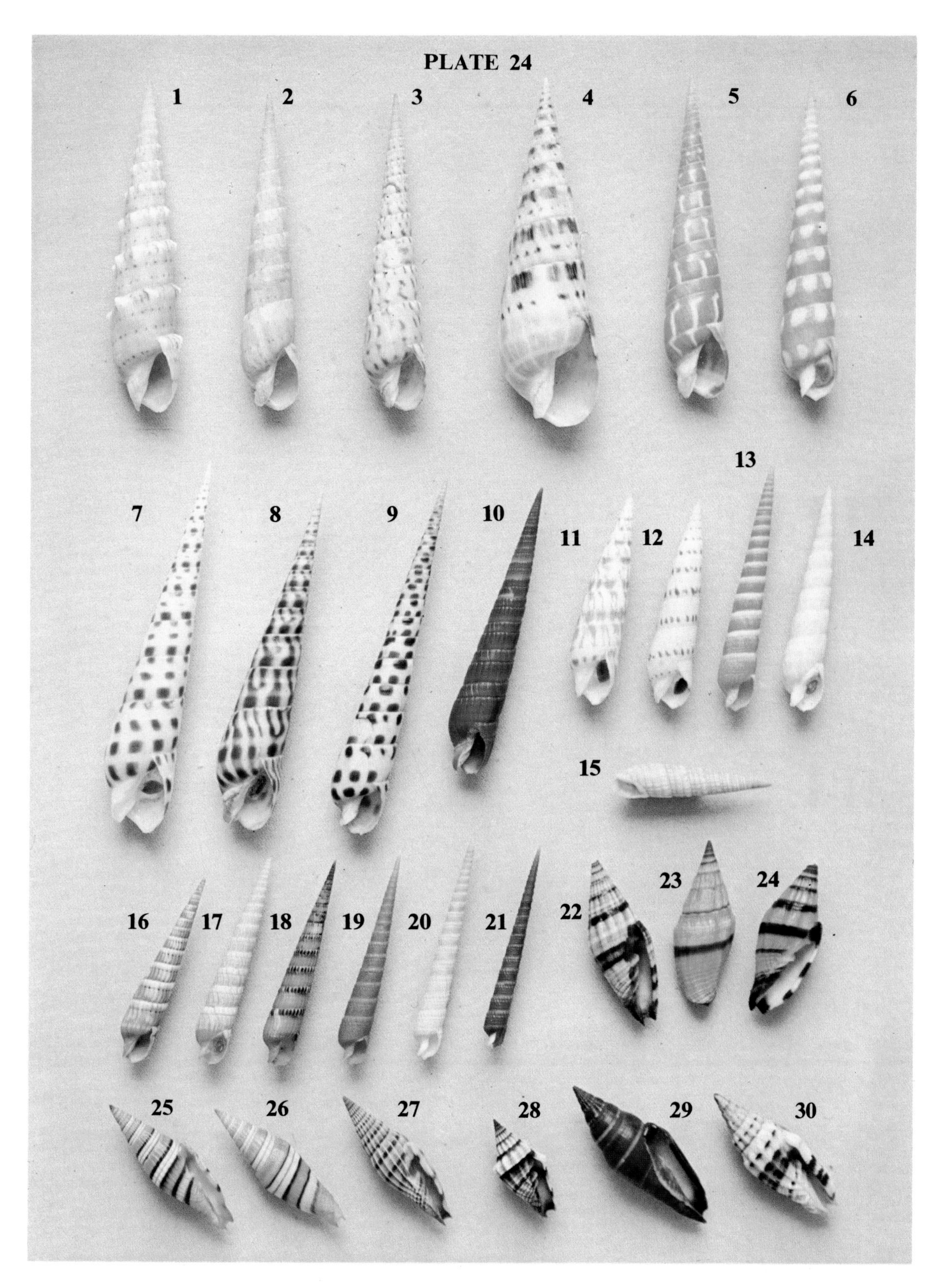
PLATE 24
1
2
3
4
5
6
7
8
9
10
11
12
13
14
15
16
17
18
19
20
21
22
23
24
25
26
27
28
29
30

FAMILY VEXILLIDAE — continued.

1. **Vexillum (Zierliana) ziervogelii** GMELIN. Port Moresby. Indo-Pacific range. Uncommon. Purplish-brown; rounded axial ribs on upper part of body whorl, spiral on lower part. Average length 25 mm.

2. **Pusia cavea** REEVE. Port Moresby. Pacific Ocean range. Uncommon. Off-white, banded with brown; narrow axial ribs. Average length 20 mm.

3. **Pusia patriarchalis** GMELIN. Port Moresby. Indo-Pacific range. Uncommon. A solid shell; white, with wide brown to black band; base orange; axial ribs and deep spiral grooves. Average length 25 mm.

4 and 5. Vexillum granosum GMELIN. Port Moresby. Indo-Pacific range. Uncommon. Blue-grey, with one or two white bands; fine axial ribs crossed by spiral grooves forming a granulose pattern; interstices purplish-brown. Average length 40 mm.

6. **Vexillum curviliratum** SOWERBY. Port Moresby. Indo-Pacific range. Scarce. Light brown, with a wide dark brown and two narrow white bands; narrow axial ribs with deep grooves in interstices. Average length 30 mm.

7 and 8. Vexillum acuminatum GMELIN. Port Moresby. Indo-Pacific range. Uncommon. Uniformly dark brown; narrow axial ribs. Average length 30 mm.

9. **Vexillum zebuense** REEVE. Siassi Islands, west New Britain. Pacific range. Uncommon. Cream, irregularly marked with brown spots, streaks, and small blotches; low axial ribs crossed by deep spiral grooves. Average length 25 mm.

10. **Vexillum acupictum** REEVE. New Britain. Indo-Pacific range. Uncommon. Similar to preceding species, but markings banded and not indiscriminate, and axial ribs more produced. Average length 25 mm.

11. **Vexillum crebriliratum** REEVE. New Britain. Ind-Pacific range. Scarce. Dark brown; fine axial ribs and deep spiral grooves. Average length 30 mm.

12. **Vexillum festum** REEVE. New Britain. Pacific Ocean range. Scarce. White, with a dark band low on body whorl; axial ribs and deep spiral grooves. Average length 25 mm.

13 to 15. Vexillum exasperatum GMELIN. Yule Island, Papua. Indo-Pacific range. Very common, and an extremely variable species. The specimens illustrated are from the one population. Average length 20 mm.

16 and 17. Vexillum sanguisugum LINNE. Rabaul, New Britain. Indo-Pacific range. Reasonably common. Dark greyish-brown, with two or three reddish bands; axial ribs cut by spiral grooves into a white beaded pattern. Average length 45 mm.

18 and 19. Vexillum gruneri REEVE. New Britain. Pacific Ocean range. Uncommon. Slate grey, with faint white bands and thin reddish-brown lines; sharp axial ribs, nodulose at shoulder, otherwise smooth. Average length 25 mm.

20. **Vexillum obeliscum** REEVE. Samarai, Papua. Indo-Pacific range. Uncommon. Brown, with two narrow white bands; numerous axial ribs and deep spiral grooves. Average length 25 mm.

21. **Vexillum cruentatum** GMELIN. New Britain. Indo-Pacific range. Uncommon. Dark brown, with white band at centre of body whorl; coarse orange coloured axial ribs; deep spiral grooves. Average length 20 mm.

22 and 23. Vexillum semifasciatum LAMARCK. Yule Island, Papua. Indo-Pacific range. Common. Cream to grey, with a broad reddish-brown band, and thin lines; ribbed axially, otherwise smooth. Average length 20 mm.

24. **Vexillum coronatum** HELBLING. Madang, New Guinea. Pacific Ocean range. Uncommon. Cream, with an orange-brown band and odd spots and blotches; axial ribs, nodulose at shoulder, with interstices spirally grooved. Averages 25 mm.

25 and 26. Vexillum cadaverosum REEVE. Bougainville Island. Indo-Pacific range. Reasonably common. Cream, with brown broken band often obsolete; axially ribbed; strongly nodulose at shoulder; fine spiral grooves. Averages 20 mm.

27. **Vexillum deshayesi** REEVE. Port Moresby. Indo-Pacific range. Common. White, with three broken brown bands; numerous axial ribs, grooved in interstices. Averages 20 mm.

28. **Vexillum costellarum** LAMARCK. New Britain. Pacific range. Uncommon. Brown, with white band at shoulder; low axial ribs and spiral grooves. Average length 30 mm.

29. **Vexillum intertaeniatum** SOWERBY. New Britain. Pacific Ocean range. Common. Blue-grey, with three to five fine brown bands and axial ribs etched with white. Averages 20 mm.

30. **Vexillum michaui** CROSSE & FISCHER. New Britain. Indo-Pacific range. Uncommon. Dark brown, with two narrow white bands, and axial ribs etched with orange-brown. Average length 20 mm.

31. **Vexillum thaanumi** PILSBRY. Tagula Island, eastern Papua. Pacific range. Scarce. White, with some obsolete brown banding; rounded axial ribs forming nodulose beads at shoulder; fine spiral grooves. Average length 20 mm.

FAMILY OLIVIDAE (introduced on Plate 26).

32. **Oliva tessellata** LAMARCK. Port Moresby. Indo-Pacific range. Common. Creamy-yellow, with purple-brown spots; aperture deep purple. Average length 25 mm.

33 to 36. Oliva oliva LINNE. A series collected on islands in the Louisiade Archipelago, eastern Papua, showing the remarkable variations in this species, even from one area. A common shell throughout the central Indo-Pacific. The only consistent characteristics are the slender cylindrical form, moderately produced spire, and the dark brown to purplish-brown aperture. Average length 32 mm.

37 and 38. Oliva rufofulgurata SCHEPMAN. Port Moresby. Western Pacific range. Uncommon. Creamy-yellow, with wavy longitudinal brown lines; aperture violet within. Average length 20 mm.

39 and 40. Oliva buloui SOWERBY. Rabaul, New Britain. Appears restricted to the New Guinea islands, where it is not common. Fusiform, with produced spire; deep yellow in colour, upper half of whorl sparsely marked, lower part with slanting reddish-brown lines and figurations. Aged specimens often with a keel-like shoulder below suture. Average length 25 mm.

41 and 42. Oliva carneola GMELIN. New Britain. Indo-Pacific range. Common. A small heavy shell with callosity covering spire; white, variably marked and banded with yellow-brown to bright orange. Odd specimens from New Britain are banded with blue-grey to mauve. Average length 20 mm.

43. **Oliva caldania** DUCLOS. Yule Island, Papua. Ranges from north Australia to South-east Asia where it is reasonably common offshore. Shell ovate; spire produced; coloured deep cream, with longitudinal zigzag brown lines. Average length 20 mm.

44 and 45. Oliva ceramensis SCHEPMAN. Dredged 40 metres, Gulf of Papua. Central Indo-Pacific range. Uncommon offshore. A small species with rounded shoulder and a callosity covering most of the short spire. Average length 15 mm.

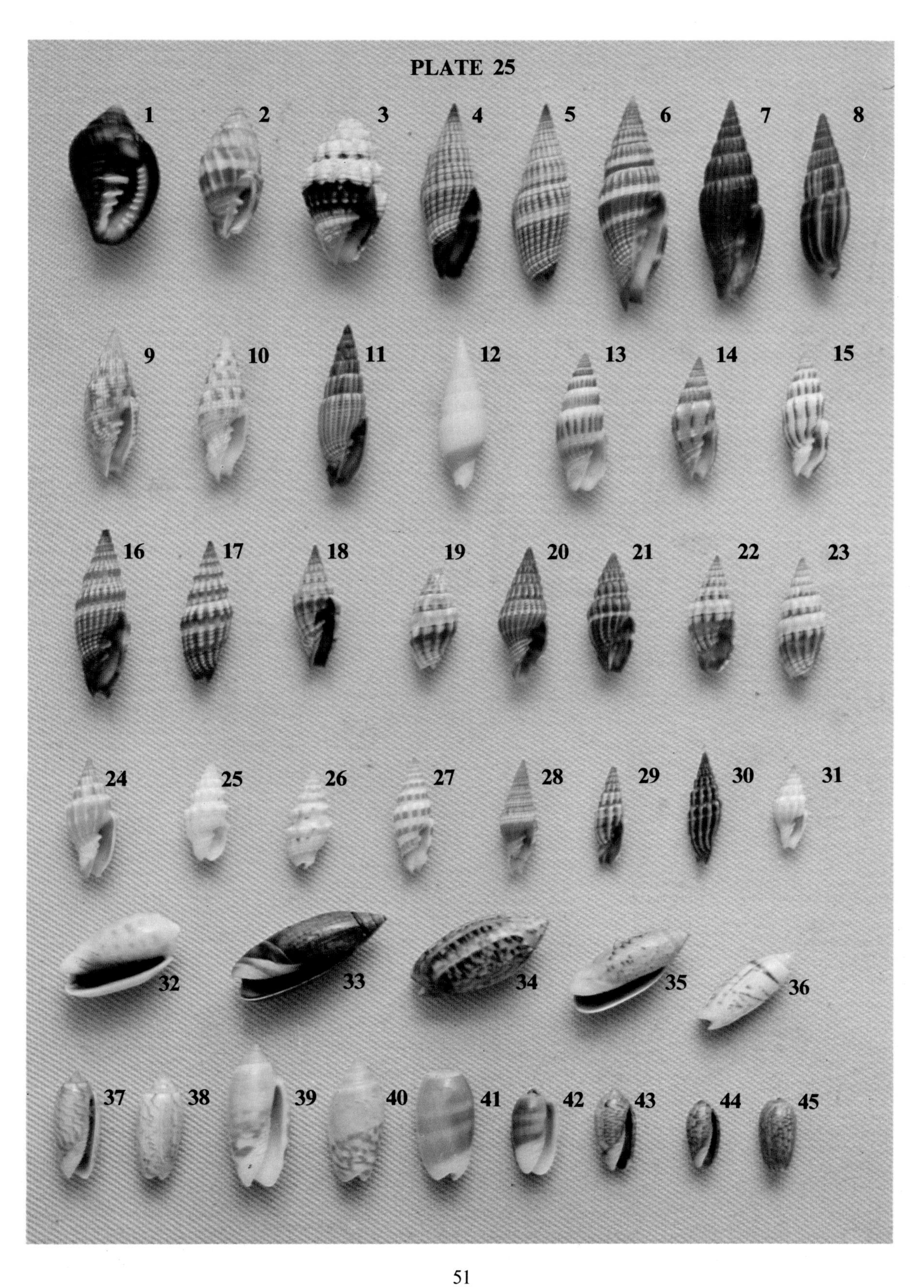
PLATE 25
1
2
3
4
5
6
7
8
9
10
11
12
13
14
15
16
17
18
19
20
21
22
23
24
25
26
27
28
29
30
31
32
33
34
35
36
37
38
39
40
41
42
43
44
45

FAMILY OLIVIDAE. Two groups of the family are well represented in the central Indo-Pacific: the true olives and the frail ancillas. The olives, with their solid, colourful, and highly polished shells, are so well known they require no descriptive introduction, but care should be exercised in their classification as some species are extremely variable in coloration and pattern. Olives are voracious carnivores. They bury in sand, and emerge at night to feed. They have no epidermis, and lack an operculum. The largest and most colourful ancillas prefer more temperate waters, but a few are found in offshore waters of tropical north Australia.

1. Ancillista velesiana IREDALE. Dredged off-shore along mid-Queensland coast. Reasonably common. A fragile shell, with rounded and inflated body whorl, and large aperture. Cream in colour, with narrow white band at sutures; spire and base of shell with broad spiral bands of rusty-brown. This is the largest and most colourful of the ancillas. Average length 90 mm.

2 to 4. Oliva miniacea RÖDING. Siassi Islands, west New Britain. Indo-Pacific range. Common. A large heavy, attractive species; very variable in colour and design, but easily recognized by its bright orange aperture. Average length 75 mm.

5. Oliva vidua RÖDING. Yule Island, Papua. Indo-Pacific range. Common. Another solid species; has low spire; wide aperture, which is bluish-white within; columella with a produced callosity posteriorly forming a slitted canal; edge of outer lip often thickened in adult specimens. Colour and pattern very variable; usually dark brown to black or olive, with two interrupted bands of darker colour. Some colour variations have a pattern similar to *O. reticulata*, while others are a uniform golden-brown or orange. These are popular with collectors. A series of these variants makes an interesting and attractive display. Average length 55 mm.

6 and 7. Oliva textilina LAMARCK. Manus Island, Admiralty Group. Distributed throughout the tropical Indo-Pacific, but is a rather rare species. A large shell; shoulders rounded; spire very short; creamy-yellow in colour, interlaced with a fine network of dark lines, usually forming an irregular and confused array of medium to small yellow triangles and spots; teeth full length of columella, and very coarse near the base; aperture a rich cream to yellow. Average length 65 mm.

8 and 9. Oliva caerulea RÖDING. Port Moresby. Indo-Pacific range. Common. A very solid shell; exserted spire; cream in colour, with brown and mauve spots often fusing into lines; aperture purple. Average length 50 mm.

10. Oliva lignaria MARRAT. North-west Australia. Central Indo-Pacific range. Reasonably common. Solid, but not heavy; moderately produced spire; cream coloured, with fine intercrossing mauve lines and two or three broken bands of light brown; aperture mauve to violet. Average length 50 mm.

11. Oliva lignaria MARRAT. Yule Island, Papua. A colour variant which is heavily blotched and streaked with dark brown.

12 and 13. Oliva reticulata RÖDING. Port Moresby. Indo-Pacific range. Common. Solid; low spire; colour variable, usually cream, densely criss-crossed with olive-brown lines, and with two darker bands; columella orange to red. Average length 40 mm.

14 and 15. Oliva annulata GMELIN. Trobriand Islands. Indo-Pacific range. Common. An attractive, solid shell with thickened outer lip; spire produced; a keel-like shoulder above centre of body whorl is present in most adult specimens; suture deeply channelled. Coloured cream to yellow, with cloudy mauve-brown spots; aperture yellow-orange. Average length 45 mm.

16 and 17. Oliva funebralis LAMARCK. Port Moresby. Central Indo-Pacific distribution. Common. A small elongate species; variable in colour and pattern; usually with a mauve-grey aperture; blue-white columella; and a small blotch of rich plum-brown on anterior extremity of fasciole. Average length 30 mm.

Note: Oliva elegans LAMARCK is another variable species, and is difficult to separate from *O. funebralis*. They are approximately the same size, and some forms are inseparable in colour and ornamentation. *O. elegans* has a paler aperture, usually bluish-white, and a pale orange tinted fasciole. There are always a few in a mixed bag of olives from New Guinea waters that could be sorted either way. Some authorities claim that *O. elegans* and small or juvenile specimens of *O. vidua* are inseparable in certain intergrading forms. Don't be disheartened if you can't classify your olives; they cause the experts to argue.

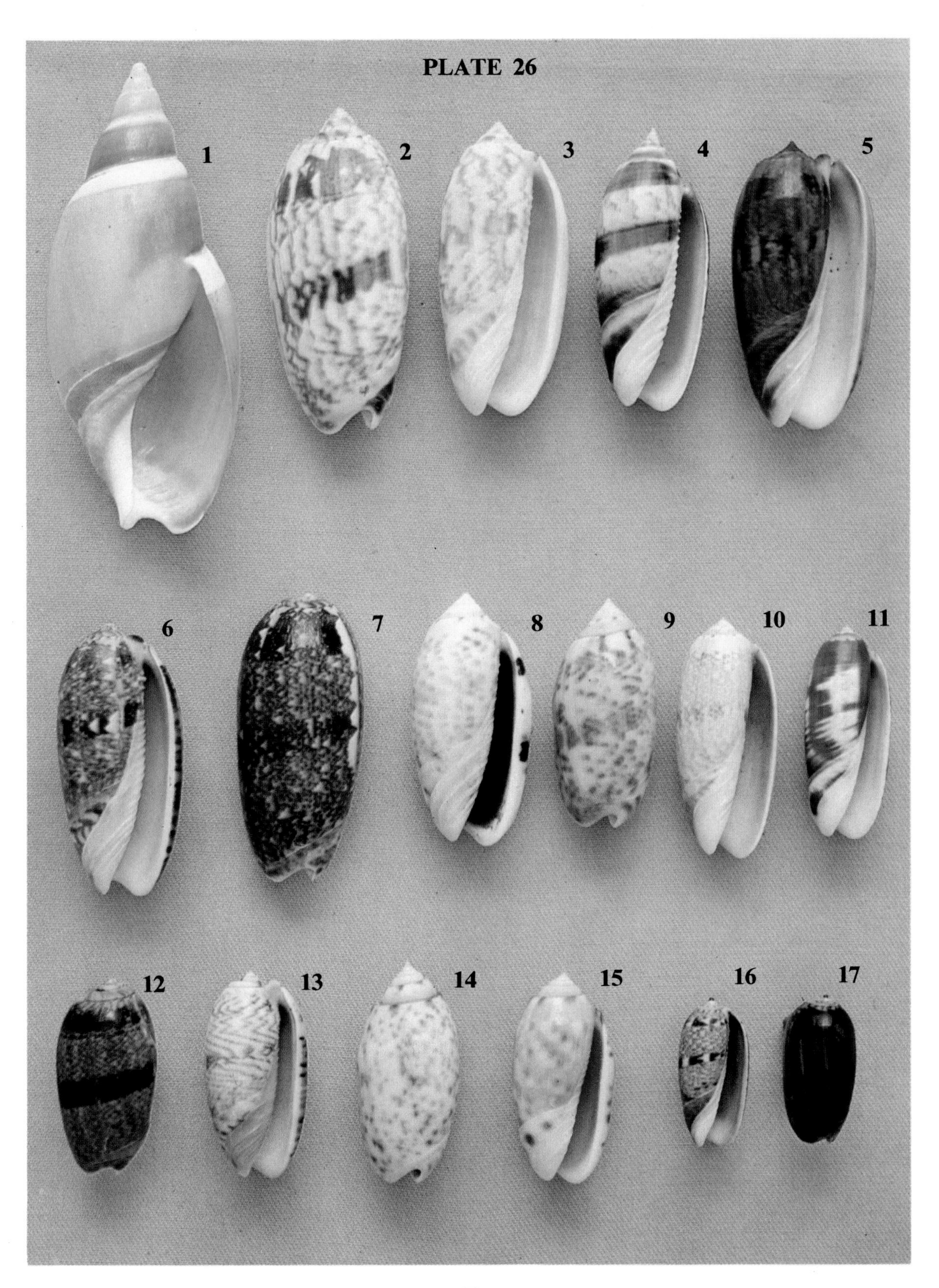
PLATE 26
1
2
3
4
5
6
7
8
9
10
11
12
13
14
15
16
17

FAMILY VOLUTIDAE. The volutes have been described by various writers as "beautiful", "noble", and "stunning". They have understandably earned these flattering descriptions. Many volutes attain a large size, and all except a few deepwater species rival the cowries and olives in their colour, ornamentation, and glossy shell surfaces. Only the rarity and consequent high cost of most volutes exclude the members of this family from the popularity to which their decorative form entitles them. Volutes hatch direct from the egg capsule at a crawling stage, so most species have a limited distribution range, tending to colonize in an area of reasonably consistent depth, or restricted by some similar ecological barrier. This colonizing tendency is undoubtedly responsible for the evolution of some small populations of volutes, obviously closely related, but with some consistent characteristics peculiar to each population, separated from their kindred neighbours by only a narrow deepwater channel. Most taxonomists fail to agree on the specific separation of these species, and, until such time as a comprehensive study of the animals is possible, and perhaps by controlled aquarium breeding, the correct classification of many species must remain in doubt. Taxonomy follows that of Weaver C. S & du Pont J. E. in *The Living Volutes* (Monograph No. 1) published by The Delaware Museum of Natural History, 1970.

1. **Melo broderipii** GRIFFITH & PIDGEON. (=*M. aethiopica* LINNE?) Trobriand Islands. Western Pacific distribution. Common. The south-east Papuan coast appears to be the southern range limit of this species. In the Gulf of Papua, the common Australian bailer, *M. amphora*, becomes evident. A cream to light brown shell, with two rows of dark brown blotches becoming obsolete bands in adult specimens. The spire is more openly exposed and the spines shorter and more numerous in this species. Average length 250 mm but attains 350 mm.
2. **Melo broderipii** GRIFFITH & PIDGEON. A freak form with a double row of spines. Collected in Siassi Islands, west New Britain.
3. **Melo broderipii** GRIFFITH & PIDGEON. A juvenile specimen from Samarai, eastern Papua, showing the similarity between this species and *M. amphora*, in young shells.
4. **Melo melo** LIGHTFOOT. Malaya. Range, South-east Asia. Reasonably common. Distinguished by its wide flaring lip and the partial sealing of the spire by the fold of the body whorl. A cream shell, with three or four broken bands of dark brown. Average length 180 mm.
5. **Melo melo** LIGHTFOOT. Dorsal view.
6. **Melo amphora** LIGHTFOOT. Gulf of Papua. Distribution, Australia to south Papuan coast. The common bailer shell. Usually with long incurving spines, often enclosing the spire; two or three rows of irregular orange-brown blotches containing some white triangular areas, and longitudinal wavy lines. Average length 300 mm. but odd specimens grow much larger.
7. **Melo amphora** LIGHTFOOT. Dorsal view.
8. **Melo amphora** LIGHTFOOT. Juvenile specimen.
9. **Cymbiola irvinae** SMITH. Restricted to north-west Australia. Scarce in good condition. A deepwater species occasionally taken in lobster pots. Apricot in colour, with some white blotches; two broad bands comprising reddish-brown spots and longitudinal lines; dark brown axial lines below sutures; shoulder with scale-like spines; aperture with five folds. Average length 115 mm.
10. **Cymbiolena magnifica** GEBAUER. Trawled off east coast of Australia. Reasonably common. A large attractive shell as its name implies. Slightly rounded nodules at shoulder; coloured cream, with bands of dark brown longitudinal blotches and triangles of creamy-white; aperture salmon to orange, with four columella plaits. Average length 230 mm.
11. **Cymbiola imperialis** LIGHTFOOT. Philippines. An uncommon shell, very popular with collectors. A large heavy species with spines at shoulder; coloured cream to pinkish, with brown longitudinal wavy lines and bands of darker colour. Average length 180 mm.
12. **Cymbiolista hunteri** IREDALE. Dredged, east coast of Australia. Common on offshore prawn grounds. A large, lightweight shell; spinose nodules at shoulder; orange to fawn in colour; ornamentation variable, usually with fine brown longitudinal wavy lines and two or three bands of squarish purple-brown blotches. Average length 150 mm.
13. **Cymbiola nobilis** SOLANDER. Malaya. Distribution — South-east Asia. Uncommon. A solid shell, with wide angular outer lip. Adult specimens with heavy callosity covering columella. Coloured cream, with zigzag longitudinal purplish-brown lines and two rows of irregular blotches. Average length 115 mm.

PLATE 27
1
2
4
3
5
6
7
8
9
10
11
12
13

FAMILY VOLUTIDAE — continued.

Figures 1 to 12 illustrate a series of volutes from the New Guinea Islands that have, for years, evaded satisfactory taxonomic classification. The island chains of eastern Papua, the Louisiade Archipelago, Trobriand Islands, New Britain, New Ireland and the Solomon Islands, all have what should be, because of the intervening deep oceans, endemic populations with distinct and separate characteristics. Some consistent locality forms do occur in each population, but, upon examining a large series from all these localities, it is frustrating and puzzling to find so many nonconformists. For instance if Nos. 2, 9, and 11 are examined, they appear to have little in common. However, a large series provides sufficient intergrading to cause serious doubt. There is no clearly defined line of differentiation. It is possible that future research and a systematic study of a large number of shells and their animals will substantiate specific splitting in some instances, and subspecific separation in others, but, until such work is completed, an attempt to apply different names at this time, will only add to the present state of confusion regarding this group of really beautiful shells.

1. Cymbiola rutila BRODERIP. Cooktown, north-east Australia. Uncommon. A solid shell; shoulder smooth or with low rounded nodules; creamy-white in colour, heavily suffused with rusty-brown to blood red, leaving some white triangular areas; a band at shoulder, and two on body whorl, of larger blotches. Aperture flesh colour to orange-brown; columella with four plaits. Average length 100 mm.

2. Cymbiola rutila BRODERIP. Samarai, eastern Papua. This form with brilliant red ornamentation is scarce. Average length 100 mm.

3. Cymbiola rutila BRODERIP. Kitava Island form. Figured specimen is ornamented with orange, and is 127 mm in length. Appears to be very scarce.

4. Cymbiola rutila BRODERIP. A form with narrow sloping shoulder angle, and produced spire, from Goodenough Island. Colouring is ginger-brown. Scarce.

5 and 6. Cymbiola rutila BRODERIP. From the Calvados Island Chain, eastern Papua. This form which has a brilliant colour pattern comprising pink, red, and dark reddish-brown, is consistent throughout this island-studded area, the only variation being in the shoulder formation which is nearly smooth in some specimens, and strongly nodulose in others. A very scarce colour form in good condition. Average length 90 mm.

7. Cymbiola rutila BRODERIP. From Samarai, eastern Papua. Colouring is nut-brown with a mauve tint, otherwise inseparable from Nos. 1 and 2. A scarce colour variant.

8. Cymbiola rutila BRODERIP. Trobriand Island form. Moderately common. White, with cream and grey blotches, and broken bands of dark brown. Average length 85 mm.

9. Cymbiola rutila BRODERIP. Laughlan Islands. This low spired, inflated form from this small isolated group of islands, appears quite distinct from all other forms. Shoulders have small spinous nodules. White in colour, finely reticulated with rusty-brown, and bands of sparse larger blotches. Very scarce. Average length 70 mm.

10. Cymbiola rutila BRODERIP. New Britain form. Shoulders consistently smoother and banding more prominent in specimens from this area. Uncommon. Average length 75 mm.

11. Cymbiola rutila BRODERIP. An unusual form from Siassi Islands, west of New Britain. Figured specimen 76 mm.

12. Cymbiola rutila BRODERIP. Lusancay Island form. Specimens from these islands are usually smaller, and have an orange-red glaze on columella and outer lip. The general colour pattern is similar to the forms from the nearby Trobriand Islands. Uncommon. Average length 55 mm.

13. Cymbiola flavicans GMELIN. Daru, western Papua. Ranges from north-west Australia to Papua. Reasonably common. Prefers inshore turbid waters, and, unlike most members of this family, often requires cleaning as adult specimens develop a hard varnish-like outer covering. With or without nodules; coloured cream, ornamented with irregular longitudinal streaks of brown, sometimes in an arrangement of bands. Aperture creamy-white. Average length 75 mm.

14 and 15. Cymbiola vespertilio LINNE. Manus Island, Admiralty Group, where it is reasonably common. Occurs only rarely in other northern New Guinea Islands, and this appears to be the southern limit to its range. A common shell in the Philippines. Extremely variable; smooth to heavily spinous; cream to pinkish, with longitudinal zigzag lines of brown or red. Aperture creamy-white. Average length 65 mm.

16. Cymbiola nivosa LAMARCK. North-west Australia, where it is reasonably common. Grey to mauve, flecked with small white triangles, and two bands of longitudinal brown lines and dashes; fine brown lines between suture and shoulder angle; interior dark brown, orange-brown near outer lip. Average length 75 mm.

17. Cymbiola nivosa LAMARCK. (= *C. oblita* E. A. Smith.) Body whorl more inflated than typical form, and with sharp spines at shoulder. Moderately common.

18 and 19. Cymbiolacca complexa IREDALE. Taken in prawn trawl nets off east coast of Australia. Moderately common. Salmon-pink to orange-brown, flecked with small white triangular spots and dotted all over with dark brown. Fine axial lines below sutures. Aperture white to flesh colour. Average length 65 mm, but odd specimens much larger.

20. Cymbiola deshayesi REEVE. New Caledonia. Uncommon. A creamy- white shell with two broad bands of red or orange blotches; aperture orange-brown. Average length 75 mm.

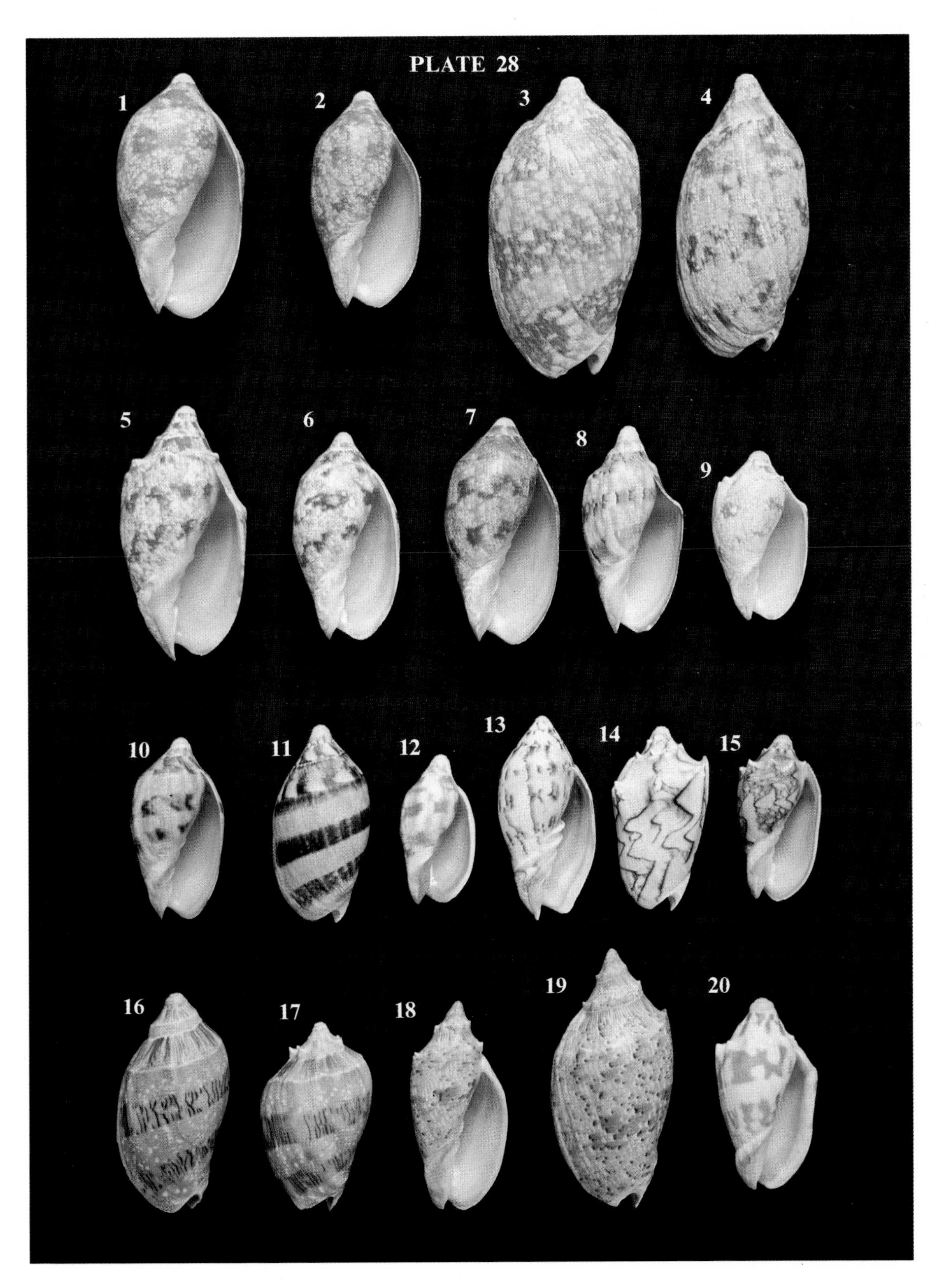
PLATE 28
1
2
3
4
5
6
7
8
9
10
11
12
13
14
15
16
17
18
19
20

FAMILY VOLUTIDAE — continued.

Most of the volutes illustrated on this plate are endemic to the east, north or north-west coast of Australia. *Volutoconus bednalli* and *Amoria turneri* occur in the Gulf of Papua.

1 to 4. Cymbiolacca pulchra SOWERBY. Variants from the north-east coast of Australia. Several names have been proposed for forms of this very variable species. Most are reasonably common at depths to 18 metres, but restricted to isolated colonies. Inshore varieties are darker in colour, usually salmon-brown, sprinkled with small white triangles, and with three bands of brown spots. Offshore specimens are cream to pale pink, with fewer spots. Average length 55 mm.

5. Cymbiolacca peristicta MCMICHAEL. Restricted to Swain's Reef, Queensland. Moderately scarce. Shell solid; sharp spines at shoulder; coloured white, with a pink or lavender tint; densely spotted over entire body whorl with reddish-brown to black. Average length 50 mm.

6. Cymbiolacca cracenta MCMICHAEL. Dredged off Townsville, north Queensland. Appears restricted to that area. Superficially resembles *C. pulchra*, but is distinguished from that species by its narrow form and darker coloration. Average length 75 mm.

7. Volutoconus bednalli BRAZIER. Dredged from 33 metres, soft mud bottom, off Yule Island, Papua. Range, north Australia to Papua. Rare. Easily distinguished by its unique colour pattern of reddish-brown to black straight spiral lines, crossed by wavy longitudinal lines of a similar colour, leaving much of the ground colour of creamy-yellow exposed. Lacks the high gloss of most volutes, but is still an outstandingly attractive species. Average length 75 mm.

8. Ericusa sericata THORNLEY. Dredged off east coast of Australia. Once very rare, now readily available from prawn trawl fishermen. A light weight, slender, smooth shell, with no shoulder angle. Creamy-fawn or pinkish, with longitudinal reticulations of light brown; obsoletely banded; aperture creamy-white. Average length 90 mm.

9. Volutoconus grossi IREDALE. Dredged north Queensland coast. Moderately rare. A smooth, slender shell; ground colour pink to orange, sprinkled with small white triangular marks, and with one or more rows of bright red blotches; aperture and columella pink, with orange patches inside outer lip. Average length 95 mm.

10. Amoria damonii GRAY. North-west Australia. Reasonably common, but one of the most beautiful of the volutes. A thin but strong shell, with large aperture. Cream, ornamented with fine axial lines and figurations of brown, with tendency to form two bands, black lines and spots below sutures; prewhorls with a rusty callosity covering most of colour pattern. Averages 100 mm.

11. Amoria molleri IREDALE. Dredged from prawn grounds off Queensland coast. Uncommon. A solid, smooth, highly polished shell. Uniform creamy-orange in colour; aperture with peculiar ridge inside and parallel to outer lip. Average length 90 mm.

12. Amoria grayi LUDBROOK. Broome, north-west Australia. Uncommon. A smooth, shiny lightweight shell, uniform cream-grey in colour; brown spots at suture, and thin slanting lines joining sutures; aperture dark brown. Average length 75 mm.

13. Amoria maculata SWAINSON. North Queensland. Uncommon. A slender, polished shell; creamy-orange in colour, with four bands of brown axial streaks; aperture light brown. Averages 75 mm.

14. Amoria maculata SWAINSON. A colour variant.

15. Amoria ellioti SOWERBY. North-west Australia. Uncommon. Shell smooth; polished; creamy-fawn, with bold, slightly wavy, axial lines; aperture brown. Average length 75 mm.

16. Amoria jamrachi GREY. North-west Australia. Uncommon. A light shell, smooth and polished; beige coloured, with thin disjointed wavy brown lines; dark spots at suture; rusty-orange callosity partly obscuring prewhorls. Average length 55 mm.

17. Amoria turneri GRIFFITH & PIDGEON. Dredged 37 metres, soft mud, off Yule Island, Papua. Ranges from north Australia to Papua. Uncommon. A light, slender, highly polished shell; cream, with close-set very thin axial brown lines, and two rows of faint mauve-brown blotches; purplish spots below sutures. Average length 45 mm.

18. Amoria praetexta REEVE. North-west Australia. Moderately rare. A small, solid, highly polished shell of a rich coffee colour with faint zigzag axial lines and two rows of irregular blotches. Average length 40 mm.

19 to 22. Amoria zebra LEACH. East coast of Australia. Common. A small heavy shell, smooth and highly polished; extremely variable in colour, and density of ornamentation. Average length 40 mm.

23. Amoria canaliculata MCCOY. Central Queensland coast. Uncommon. A smooth highly polished shell; deep channels at sutures; white to pink, with fine pink axial lines, and rows of orange-brown squarish blotches. Average length 50 mm.

24. Ternivoluta studeri VON MARTENS. From deep water off east Australian coast. Common. A lightweight shell; sharply angled at shoulder, spinous in some specimens; cream to fawn in colour, with fine axial lines and three rows of irregular figurations. Average length 50 mm.

25. Nannamoria parabola GARRARD. Dredged from deep water, south Queensland. Moderately rare. A small, solid shell; not polished; axial ribs or folds becoming sharply spinous at shoulder; fawn coloured, with fine brown longitudingal lines and two rows of reddish-brown blotches. Average length 30 mm.

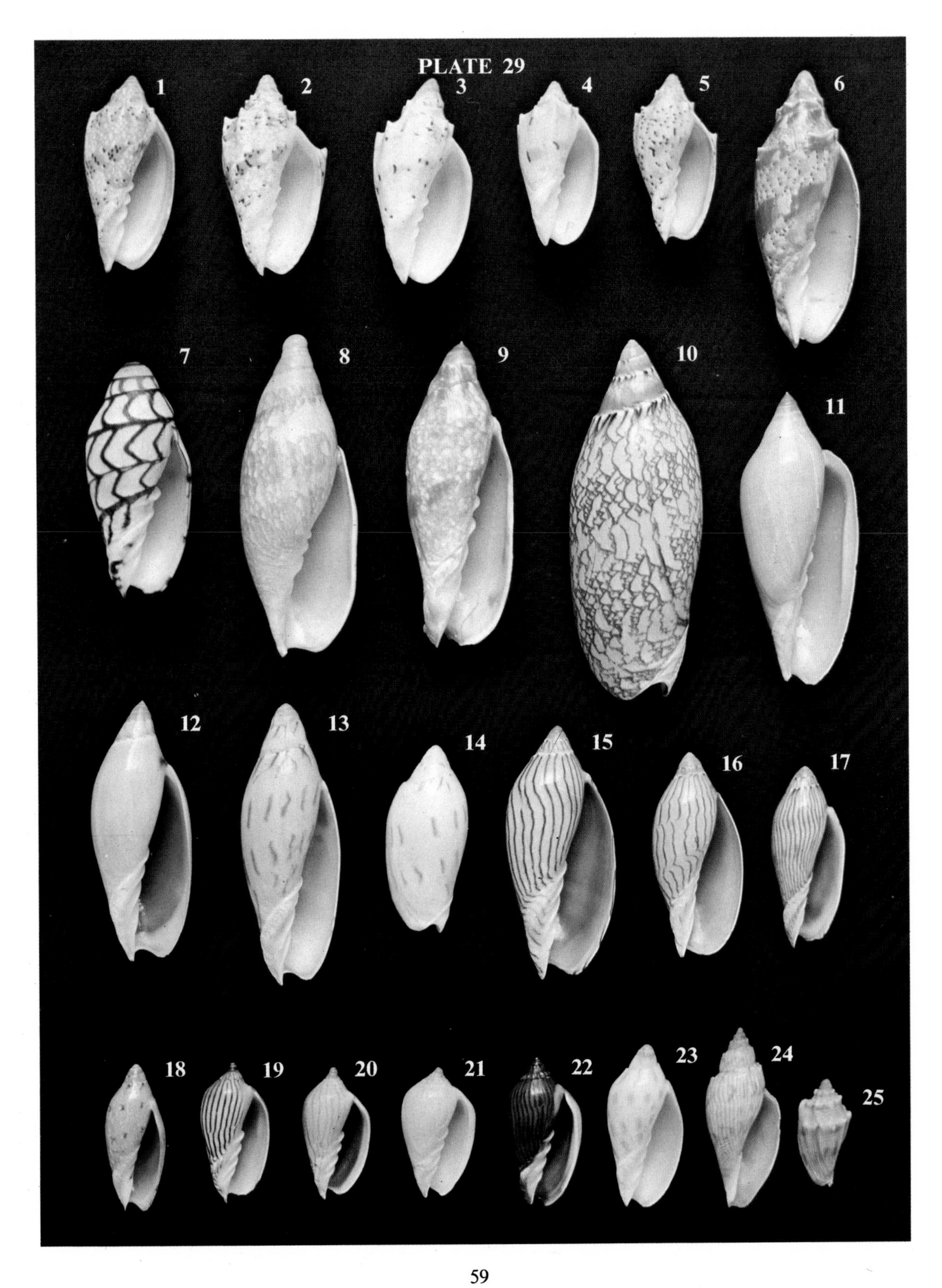
PLATE 29
1
2
3
4
5
6
7
8
9
10
11
12
13
14
15
16
17
18
19
20
21
22
23
24
25

FAMILY TURRIDAE. The turrid shells include several hundred species, but comparatively few attain sufficient size to attract the attention of collectors. This plate illustrates some of the larger forms likely to be encountered in the tropical central Indo-Pacific. The turrids are variable in form and sculpture, the consistent characteristic being the presence of a well defined slit or sinus in the upper part of the outer lip. In general appearance the turrids resemble members of the family Fasciolariidae, but are actually related to the cones and terebras.

1. **Turris crispa** LAMARCK. Dredged 18 metres Port Moresby Harbour. Distribution — Indo-Pacific. Common. A large species; white, with dark brown spots often arranged in a longitudinal pattern; decorated with spiral ridges separated by two or three spiral cords. Proportionately narrower than *T. babylonia.* Average length 100 mm.
2. **Turris babylonia** LINNE. Port Moresby. Range restricted to central Indo-Pacific. Common. A solid shell; creamy-white, with rows of dark brown to black spots on the raised spiral ribs; interstices between ribs with two or three fine cords. Average length 75 mm.

3 to 5. **Lophiotoma indica** RÖDING. 37 metres off Yule Island, Gulf of Papua. Distribution — Indonesia and Australia to Fiji. Uncommon offshore. Colour variable as indicated in forms illustrated. Sculpturing consists of numerous smooth spiral ridges and fine spiral cords; one prominent ridge on each whorl bearing larger brown maculations; anterior canal long and straight. Average length 75 mm.

6. **Turris undosa** LAMARCK. 18 metres Port Moresby Harbour. Distribution — central Indo-Pacific. An uncommon and attractive species; distinguished by its tall spire, short canal and mauve to violet aperture. A white shell densely marked with brown often forming a wavy longitudinal pattern. Average length 75 mm.
7. **Gemmula unedo** KIENER. 27 metres, Yule Island, Gulf of Papua. Distribution, central Indo-Pacific. An uncommon offshore species. Creamy-white decorated with numerous spiral ribs becoming corded towards base; concave between suture and shoulder; spiral ribs with orange-brown spots arranged in longitudinal pattern, and some orange-fawn zones on whorl. Average length 65 mm.
8. **Gemmula gilchristi** SOWERBY. 22 metres, Port Moresby Harbour. Distribution — central Indo-Pacific. Uncommon. A small light brown shell, whitish near base and on anterior canal; anterior canal distinctly curved; numerous spiral cords, the three stronger cords at shoulder angle are crossed by regularly spaced vertically elongate nodules in a cog-like pattern. Averages 40 mm.
9. **Gemmula speciosa** REEVE. 37 metres, off Yule Island, Gulf of Papua. Distribution, central Indo-Pacific. Uncommon. A creamy-white shell; decorated with numerous sharply raised ridges coloured light brown, and a row of short axially elongate nodules at shoulder in a cog-like pattern; siphonal canal long and recurved. Average length 65 mm.
10. **Turricula javana** LINNE. 46 metres, Yule Island, Papua. Distribution — South-east Asia to New Guinea. Uncommon. Uniform buff to light brown; distinctive oblique white nodules at shoulder, and numerous fine axial ridges and fine raised lines; anterior canal recurved with extremity expanded. Average length 65 mm.
11. **Xenuroturris cingulifera** LAMARCK. 40 metres, Yule Island, Papua. Distribution — Indo-Pacific. Reasonably common. Easily recognized by its tall spire and very short anterior canal. Coloured cream to fawn, with a row of brown spots on shoulder ridge and profusely marked on the numerous lesser spiral cords with brown dots and dashes. Average length 50 mm.
12. **Turricula nelliae** E. A. SMITH. 33 metres, Yule Island, Papua. Distribution — Indian Ocean to China, New Guinea and Australia. Uncommon. Coarsely sculptured with prominent gemmate spiral ridges and a row of slightly oblique and axially elongate nodules at shoulder; coloured cream to fawn with brown blotches and spots between raised nodules; siphonal canal medium in length and slightly recurved. Average length 30 mm.
13. **Leucosyrinx queenslandica** POWELL. 46 metres, Yule Island, Gulf of Papua. Previously recorded from deep water off southern Queensland. Live specimens are scarce. A slender attractive species with a tall spire; angulate at shoulder; concave at shoulder slope; siphonal canal long, thin and reasonably straight; shell comparatively smooth, spiral ridges being fine and low, with one row of prominent nodules at shoulder; coloured cream to fawn variably and profusely maculated with reddish-brown. Averages 50 mm.
14. **Lophiotoma acuta** PERRY. 37 metres, Gulf of Papua, Distribution — Indo-Pacific. Reasonably common offshore. A narrow shell; tall spire; moderately long siphonal canal, slightly curved; densely sculptured with fine spiral grooves and ridges becoming gemmate at base, and a pair of prominent smooth ridges at shoulder; coloured cream, profusely sprinkled with medium to minute dark brown spots. Average length 45 mm.
15. **Clathrodrillia flavidula** LAMARCK. 37 metres, Yule Island. Spire tall; siphonal canal short and recurved; uniform white to cream; low oblique longitudinal fold-like ribs crossed by numerous spiral ridges; whorls rounded, only slightly angulate at shoulder. Figured specimen 57·15 mm.
16. **Inquisitor** species. 40 metres, Yule Island. A small strongly sculptured shell; longitudinal folds crossed by fine spiral raised ribs; spire tall; siphonal canal short; brown in colour, the spiral ridges etched with cream. Figured specimen 31·75 mm.
17. **Inquisitor** species. 119 metres off Caloundra, south Queensland. A fawn to brown shell; strong, slightly oblique axial folds of a creamy-white colour, crossed by rounded spiral ridges; siphonal canal short and tinted with lavender. Figured specimen 28·6 mm.
18. **Inquisitor solomonensis** E. A. SMITH. 26 metres, Rabaul Harbour. A narrow, solid shell; short siphonal canal; rounded longitudinal ridges more prominent at the angulate shoulder, the interstices are dark brown and spirally grooved; remainder of shell light brown. Figured specimen 25·4 mm.
19. **Clavus canicularis** RÖDING. Port Moresby, intertidal to a few metres depth. Distribution — Indo-Pacific. Common. A small solid shell; whitish, with a broad reddish-brown band; strongly spinous nodules at shoulder. Average length 25 mm.
20. **Clavus unizonata** LAMARCK. Siassi Island, west New Britain. Distribution — central Indo-Pacific. Uncommon. A small bluish-grey shell, with one dark band on whorl; raised axial folds, most prominent at shoulder. Average length 20 mm.

PLATE 30
1
2
3
4
5
6
7
8
9
10
11
12
13
14
15
16
17
18
19
20

FAMILY CONIDAE. Cone shells are, taxonomically, one of the most difficult of all groups of marine shells. There are nearly 1,500 names proposed for living species, but most researchers today consider that as few as 400 to 450 are valid.

The mass of synonymy resulting from the variations in many species is most confusing to the amateur collector, and a problem to the professional taxonomist. Range and clinal variations create problems in several families of shells, but some cones appear in a diversity of colour and form even in the one population.

Members of this family range in size from 6 mm to 230 mm in length. Some are light in weight with fragile outer lips, and others are solid and heavy. All are conical in shape; some have a tall tapering or stepped spire, others are flat or even slightly depressed. In most species the aperture is long and narrow; the columella and outer lip is smooth and simple. All cones possess a horny operculum, which is oval and minute in *Conus omaria*; large and narrowly elongate, almost half the length of the aperture, in such species as *C. miles* and *C. vexillum*.

In life, all cones are covered with an epidermis or periostracum, which may be thin, smooth, and transparent; thick and velvety; or tufted. Some species are ornamented with beautiful colour patterns when the epidermis is removed, others are delicately and evenly grooved and sculptured.

The tropical waters of the Indo-Pacific Province are rich in cone shells. Most species have a wide distribution and are reasonably abundant. A few are very scarce and rival the cowries and volutes in popularity, and are expensive items to procure through dealers.

In the following text, subgeneric classification has been avoided, and all species have been referred to under the broad genus *Conus*. In a family of shells which includes some 400 or more distinct species, division into subgenera would be an obvious advantage, but the present organization is is need of revision. In view of recent anatomical studies, the divisions based merely on shell characters are inadequate and confusing.

The radular teeth of cone shells have developed or evolved into a most efficient venom apparatus with which the mollusc can inject into the victim a paralyzing or lethal dose of venom. The potency and reaction of the poison vary according to the food preference of each species of *Conus*. Anatomical studies and observations of feeding habits of live specimens in aquaria indicate that cones may be divided into three groups: (a) Piscivorous species, which kill and eat fish. These are dangerous to all vertebrates, including man. *C. geographus* is the most notorious of this group, having caused several deaths. *C. striatus*, *C. magus*, *C. stercusmuscarum*, and *C. tulipa* are other piscivorous species, and *C. monachus* and *C. catus* are suspect. (b) Molluscivorous species, which eat molluscs including other cone shells. *C. textile* and related tent cones are molluscivorous. *C. textile* has a nasty reputation, having inflicted several injuries on humans, and some deaths have been reported. (c) Vermivorous species, which prefer small marine worms. *C. litteratus*, *C. eburneus*, and *C. betulinus* are examples of this group. They are not considered dangerous to man, but their sting would probably cause some pain and discomfort.

After stunning, the cone shell draws its victim into its expandable proboscis sheath where digestion takes place. Piscivorous species regurgitate a mucous-enshrouded bundle of bones and fatty substances some six hours after digestion commences. The vermivorous species, *C. litteratus*, will sometimes disgorge worms after they have been collected. *C. textile* are particularly partial to the smaller forms of strombs, and have been observed injecting three darts to subdue a victim completely. This molluscivorous species then uses its muscular foot to help draw the dead animal from the shell, while its proboscis sheath completely or partially envelops the soft tissues. Occasionally two textile cones will feed together on the one mollusc.

Until more is known of the feeding habits of cone shells, and research gives a better understanding of the venomology of this genus, all cone shells should be treated with respect. Collectors are advised to exercise the utmost caution when handling all live specimens of cones. **It is definitely not safe to hold cone shells by the shoulder or posterior end.** At least four species have been observed to extend their flexible proboscis, which holds a radular dart in readiness, well beyond the shoulder level of their own shell. This capability has been noted in the piscivorous species *C. geographus*, *C. striatus*, and *C. magus* and in the common molluscivorous species *C. textile*. Use a glove to pick up cone shells and do not handle them again while they are alive. *C. geographus*, *C. textile*, and *C. omaria* become very active and aggressive when they have been removed from their natural environment, and are more likely to inflict an injury some hours after collection.

Note: The application of heat to the cone shell greatly reduces the potency of the venom, but if frozen, even for prolonged periods, the venom remains dangerous. So collectors should use the utmost caution when removing the animal from frozen-preserved shells. A few minutes boiling will not spoil the shell and may prevent a great deal of discomfort and distress.

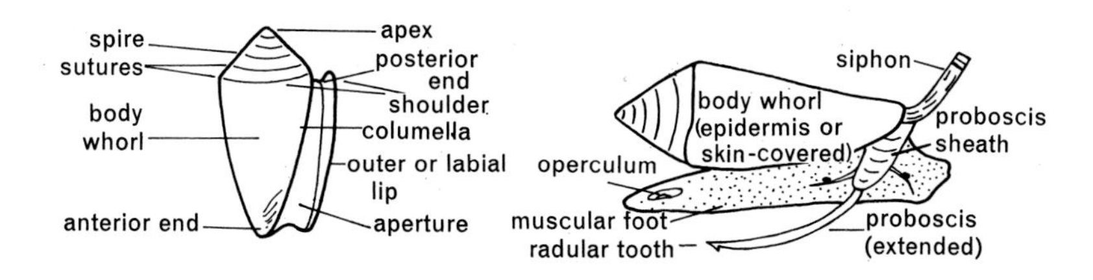

FAMILY CONIDAE.

1. **Conus marmoreus** LINNE. Port Moresby. Indo-Pacific range. Common. An attractive species featuring much variation in colour ornamentation over its distributional range. This is the typical form. A stout shell; coronated; sides comparatively straight; coloured white, with brown to black reticulations forming triangular whitish spots; sometimes with a pink tint inside aperture. Average length 75 mm.

Several of the following forms illustrated on this plate have been given specific names. A few are recognized today, but most are considered to be either genetic or range variations, and a more thorough examination of many specimens, including intergrading forms, is indicated before they can be justifiably separated.

2. **Conus marmoreus** LINNE. A form with heavy longitudinal reticulations from New Britain.

3. **Conus marmoreus** LINNE. Form from New Caledonia.

4 and 5. Conus marmoreus LINNE (*bandanus* HWASS). This form is distinguished from typical *C. marmoreus* by the presence of two banded zones of darker coloration on the body whorl. No. 5 illustrates the obvious intergradation with the typical form. Average length 75 mm.

6. **Conus marmoreus** LINNE (*bandanus*). Trobriand Islands. This is an example of one of several species of cones occurring in a dwarf or stunted form in the islands off eastern Papua. Average length 25 mm.

7. **Conus nicobaricus** HWASS. Philippines. Two narrow dark zones leaving three bands of pale, sometimes indistinct, reticulated ornamentation. A large shell, averaging 75 mm in length.

8. **Conus vidua** REEVE. Philippines. Uncommon. A stout shell, with two vivid dark brown to blackish bands. Average length 65 mm.

9 and 10. Conus marmoreus LINNE. Manus Island, Admiralty Group. Ranges from New Guinea to Fiji. A melanistic form of *C. marmoreus*. Inside of aperture usually bright pink. Average length 50 mm.

11. **C. marmoreus** LINNE. An albinistic form from New Caledonia, where it is moderately rare. Average length 50 mm. See also Plate 34, No. 12.

12. **Conus marmoreus** LINNE (*crosseanus* BERNARDI). Another distinct variation restricted to New Caledonia. Scarce. Smaller than typical form, with a blue-grey tint over the white base colour. Average length 40 mm.

13. **Conus zonatus** HWASS. Maldive Island, Indian Ocean. A rare species restricted to east Indian Ocean area. Usually disfigured with healed scars indicating its habitat is associated with exposed or semi-exposed ocean reefs. Average length 50 mm.

14. **Conus stercusmuscarum** LINNE. Port Moresby. Central Indo-Pacific range. Reasonably common. A piscivorous species. Shell solid; sides rounded; shoulder smooth; concave between sutures; aperture wide, vividly coloured deep orange within; body whorl white, peppered with small dark brown dots and some irregular blotches. Average length 50 mm.

15 and 16. Conus pulicarius HWASS. Port Moresby. Indo-Pacific range. A common sand-dwelling species. A solid, coronated shell, consistent in shape but variable in colour and degree of ornamentation. Typical form is white, with some yellow banding and irregular dark brown to black dots. Figure 16 is an extremely dark form. Odd forms are found that are uniformly white. Average length 40 mm.

17. **Conus arenatus** HWASS. Port Moresby. Indo-Pacific range. Common in sand. A solid little coronated shell, white in colour, densely ornamented with minute brown spots, sometimes massed into squarish blotches, and arranged in wavy axial figurations. Average length 40 mm.

18. **Conus arenatus** HWASS. Samarai, Papua. A pustulose or granulated form.

PLATE 31
1
2
3
4
5
6
7
8
9
10
11
12
13
14
15
16
17
18

FAMILY CONIDAE — continued.

1 to 4. Conus imperialis LINNE. A series of specimens from the New Guinea Islands illustrating the consistency of form, but the diversity in coloration of this handsome species of cone shell which is reasonably abundant throughout the Indo-Pacific. The shoulders are strongly coronated; spire low to flat; sides comparatively straight; spiral cords at base of shell becoming obsolete higher on body whorl; aperture narrow; outer lip thin. Average length 65 mm.

5. Conus bullatus LINNE. Manus Island, Admiralty Group. Distribution restricted to central Indo-Pacific. A rare and colourful species. The rounded sides, sloping shoulder angle, small partly depressed spire, flaring aperture, and the high gloss and colouring of this cone make it readily distinguishable from all other members of the family. Superficially it resembles an olive shell. Specimens from the Louisiade Archipelago in eastern Papua are proportionately narrower, with bright reddish banding on body whorl. Average length 50 mm.

6. Conus spectrum LINNE. North-west Australia. Ranges, in variable colour forms, throughout the central Indo-Pacific. Uncommon. A lightweight shell, with a wide aperture and thin lip; creamy-white, ornamented with irregular rusty-brown blotches and longitudinal streaks. Average length 45 mm.

7. Conus spectrum LINNE. Deepwater form from Queensland coast.

8. Conus spectrum LINNE. From Broome, Western Australia. Often placed in collections under the name *C. stillatus*.

9. Conus spectrum LINNE. Dredged off mid-Queensland coast. Average length 40 mm. Of a lighter coloration and consistently smaller size than typical *C. spectrum*.

10 and 11. Conus pica A. ADAMS & REEVE. Colour forms from Borneo. Another species closely related to *C. spectrum*, and may be another form of that variable species. Average length 30 mm.

12. Conus radiatus GMELIN. Dredged Port Moresby Harbour. Range, south-west Pacific. Moderately common offshore. Uniformly brown in colour, except for a whitish band at shoulder. Lower part of body whorl with widely spaced spiral grooves, smooth on upper part; prominent axial growth lines. Average length 50 mm.

13. Conus radiatus GMELIN. A narrow, pale coloured form from 54 metres, off Oro Bay, north coast of Papua.

14. Conus radiatus GMELIN. Dark form from New Britain.

15 and 16. Conus carinatus SWAINSON. New Britain. Central Indo-Pacific range. Considered by some authorities to be one of the rarer forms of *C. magus*, but retained by others as a "good" species. One consistent differentiating characteristic is the dark apical point on the spire. Average length 50 mm.

17 and 18. Conus parius REEVE. New Britain. Range, Philippines to New Guinea. Uncommon. Varies in colour from fawn to dark brown, with the sharp apex stained dark brown to black. Average length 30 mm.

19 to 24. Conus ochroleucus GMELIN. New Britain. South-west Pacific distribution. Moderately rare over most of its restricted distributional range, but fairly abundant in east New Britain. The growth series illustrated here gives some indication of the variations in certain species of cones, particularly between the juveniles and adults. The juvenile forms figured here are sharply angulate at the shoulder, with deep spiral grooves over entire body whorl; cream in colour, with longitudinal streaks and blotches of reddish-brown; aperture white. Fully adult specimens are rounded at the shoulder line; grooved on lower part of body whorl only; uniformly ochreous-yellow in colour, except on the spire which retains the brown markings of earlier growth stages; the aperture is a deep yellow inside. Average length of adult shells is 55 mm.

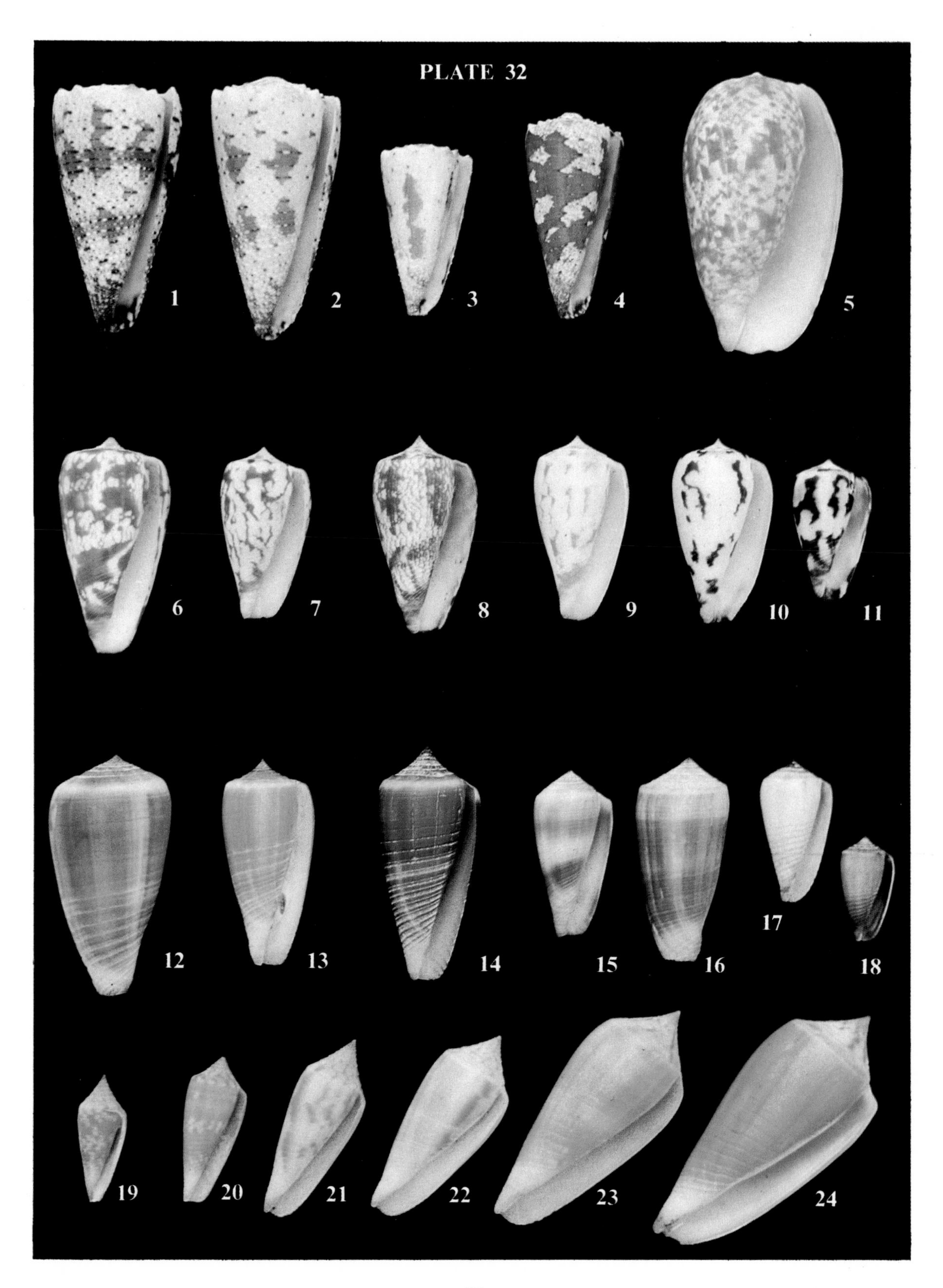
PLATE 32
1
2
3
4
5
6
7
8
9
10
11
12
13
14
15
16
17
18
19
20
21
22
23
24

FAMILY CONIDAE — continued.

1 to 5. Conus eburneus HWASS. A series of colour variations from the New Guinea Islands. A common sand-dwelling species, with a long narrow operculum. Periostracum thin, smooth, light brown. Average length 40 mm, but odd specimens grow much larger.

6. Conus caracteristicus FISCHER. A solid, medium sized shell, restricted to South-east Asia and Philippine Islands, where it is reasonably common, and consistent in form and coloration. A shallow water species. Periostracum smooth, brown. Average length 45 mm.

7. Conus tessulatus BORN. Samarai, eastern Papua. Indo-Pacific range. Common. An attractive species, with some variation in the density of the spirally elongate, orange coloured spots on a white ground. Has a short but sharp spire; aperture pink to light lavender; periostracum thin, smooth, yellow-brown. Intertidal to several fathoms depth. Average length 45 mm.

8. Conus tessulatus BORN. A chunky form with large squarish, orange-red blotches. From Rabaul, New Britain.

9. Conus flavidus LAMARCK. Port Moresby. Indo-Pacific range. A common species. Shoulder smooth; body whorl obsoletely grooved in adult specimens; axial growth lines, becoming prominent with age; periostracum coarse, dark brown. Inhabits the intertidal zones. Average length 50 mm.

10. Conus flavidus LAMARCK. Port Moresby. A juvenile specimen, lacking the deep orange coloration of the adult shell, and with punctate spiral grooves on lower part of body whorl.

11. Conus flavidus LAMARCK. Port Moresby. A colour variant with two white bands at centre of body whorl.

12 to 15. Conus distans HWASS. Samarai, eastern Papua. Indo-Pacific range. Common. Shoulder and prewhorls with prominent white nodules. Adult specimens a uniform brown with some blue-grey zoning, and an obsolete white band; prominent axial growth lines. Prefers shallow exposed coral reef platforms. The juvenile shells (No. 12 and No. 13), which appear to remain in deeper water, are scarce. These are beautifully marked, and bear little resemblance to the adult shell. They have widely spaced deep spiral grooves. Periostracum thin, semi-transparent, with rows of raised fin-like tufts, but comparatively smooth in aged forms. Average length 75 mm.

16. Conus parvulus LINK. Port Moresby. Western Pacific range. Reasonably common. Rounded white nodules at shoulder, with dark brown spot between nodules; angular spiral ridges; fine growth lines; coloured light brown with mauve zones, and white band at centre. Anterior end purplish-brown. Small oval operculum, and dark brown periostracum. Average length 30 mm.

17. Conus parvulus LINK. Dark form from north Queensland.

18 to 20. Conus clarus SMITH. North-west Australia. Distribution — Western Australia to south-east Africa. Uncommon. Typical form has flat spire with sharp apical point; body whorl comparatively smooth; coloured white to yellow-brown; rusty-brown stain at base; and radiating brown lines on spire. Average length 40 mm.

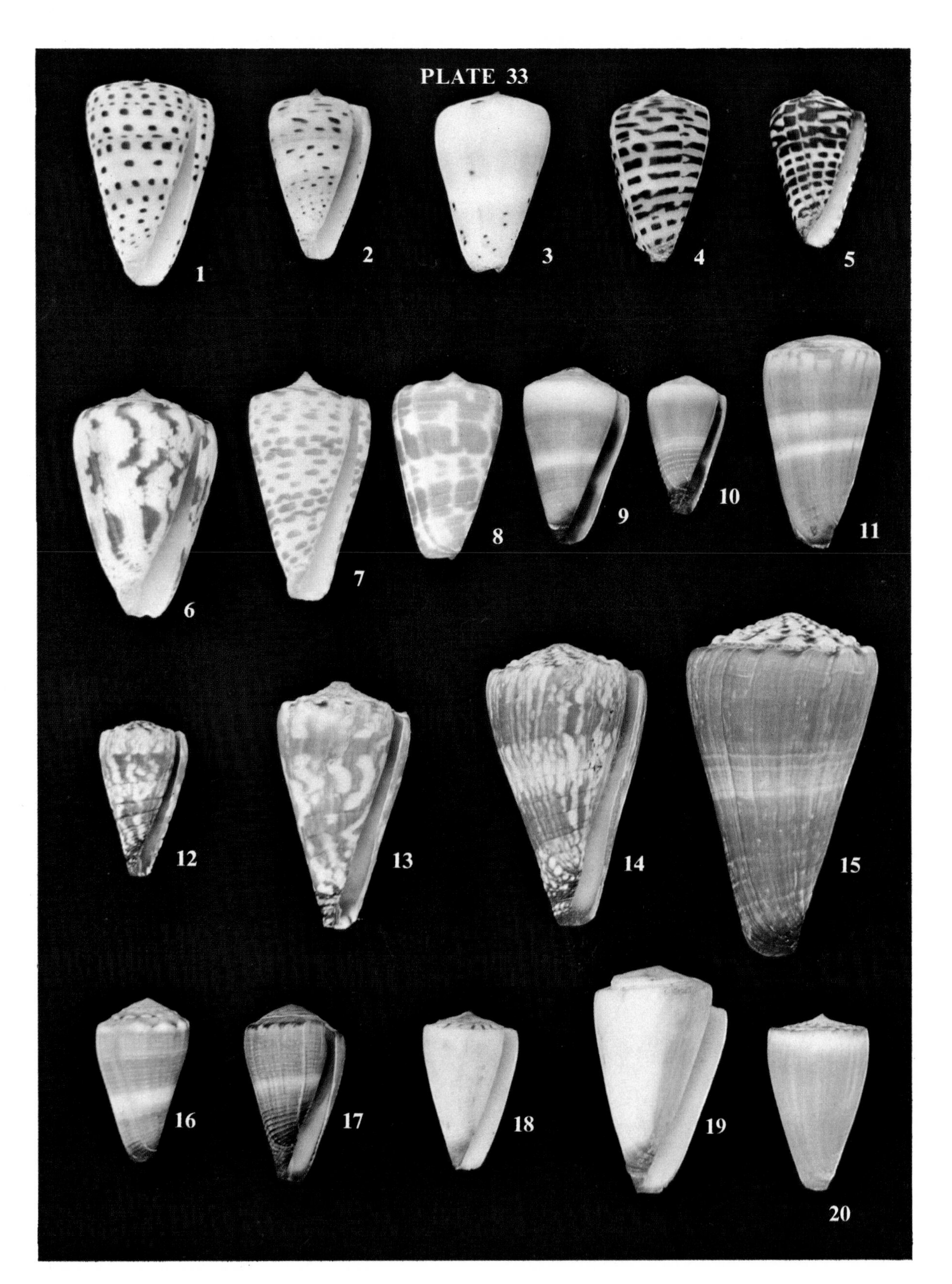
PLATE 33
1
2
3
4
5
6
7
8
9
10
11
12
13
14
15
16
17
18
19
20

FAMILY CONIDAE — continued.

1. **Conus litteratus** LINNE. Samarai, Papua. Indo-Pacific range. Common. A large polished shell when the thick brown velvety periostracum is removed; shoulder sharply angulate; spire flat or slightly depressed; sides comparatively straight; aperture narrow; white in colour, with yellow bands, and marked with dark brown to black squarish spots in spiral bands; base of shell stained purplish-black. Average length 130 mm, but grows larger.
2. **Conus leopardus** RÖDING. Trobriand Islands, Papua. Indo-Pacific range. Common. A very large and heavy shell with a dull surface texture; shoulder slightly rounded; spire low and rounded; sides comparatively straight; aperture narrow; off-white in colour, with dark grey, sometimes cloudy, spots in spiral bands; base of shell unmarked. Average length 165 mm, but grows larger.
3. **Conus virgo** LINNE. Port Moresby. Indo-Pacific range. Common. A large solid species; spire low to medium height; sides straight; aperture narrow; fine spiral grooves and axial growth lines; young shells uniformly light yellow becoming white in mature specimens; base of shell with purple stain. Average length 90 mm.
4. **Conus emaciatus** REEVE. Port Moresby. Indo-Pacific range. Common. A medium sized, heavy shell; low spire; sides concave hence the name *emaciatus*; strong spiral ridges sometimes corded, and weak axial growth lines; aperture narrow; uniformly yellow-orange in colour, with purple blotch at base. Average length 50 mm.
5. **Conus coelinae** CROSSE. New Caledonia, to which area it appears restricted. Moderately rare. A highly polished shell; white to flesh colour; close-set fine spiral lines; shoulder sharply angulate; spire low; sides straight, tapering to narrow base which is tinted lavender; aperture narrow. Average length 50 mm.
6. **Conus sugimotonis** KURODA. Dredged 183 metres south Queensland coast. Range, Japan to Australia. Rare in live condition. Adult specimens uniformly white, with a small brown stain at base; shoulder sharply angulate, though somewhat rounded below; spire low, with sharp apex; sides slightly concave; aperture comparatively narrow; outer lip frail; body whorl smooth except for numerous fine and coarse axial growth lines. Figured specimen 82·55 mm.
7. **Conus recluzianus** BERNARDI. Dredged 145-180 metres, south Queensland. Range — Japan to east Australia. Rare. Narrower than preceding species; white in colour, with two indistinct bands of brown markings, becoming obsolete in aged specimens; shoulder sharply angulate with low crenulations; spire flat, with sharp apex; sides straight: aperture very narrow; outer lip curved and very frail; fine spiral grooves and coarser axial growth lines. Figured specimen 69·85 mm.
8. **Conus recluzianus** BERNARDI. Dredged off Taiwan. An extremely variable species regarding coloration with the result that many names have been applied to this cone shell. Usually the juveniles are more brilliantly decorated and become less colourful in later growth stages. Occasionally, as in this instance, a larger specimen retains the decorative markings, causing some confusion. This specimen has granular cords on lower half of body whorl and is smooth with fine spiral lines on upper part; aged shells with coarse axial growth lines. Figured specimen 82·55 mm, but attains 100 mm.
9. **Conus sieboldi** REEVE. Japan. Range, China Seas. Reasonably common. A tall slender and graceful species; white in colour, with irregular brown blotches usually arranged in two bands; shoulder angulate; spire produced to a sharply pointed apex, stepped and channelled; sides narrowed or concave; aperture moderately narrow; outer lip frail and gracefully curved; deep spiral grooves on lower part of body whorl, smooth above. Averages 75 mm.
10. **Conus stupa** KURODA (*stupella* KURODA). Dredged 240 metres off Taiwan. Range, China Seas. Very rare. A white shell, with several spiral rows of reddish-brown dots; biconic in shape, with a high prominently stepped spire; sides tapering from a broad shoulder to be very narrow at anterior end; aperture narrow. Figured specimen 63·5 mm.
11. **Conus teramachii** KURODA. Dredged 274 metres, Japan. Range — China Seas. A rare species. A large shell, uniformly fawn to light brown; shoulder with an unusual ridge, slightly corded; spire tall, stepped; prominent spiral grooves at base of body whorl, but only fine lines above; aperture moderately wide, and cream to yellow within; outer lip curved and frail. Figured specimen 88·9 mm.
12. **Conus marmoreus** LINNE (albino form). Restricted to New Caledonia, where it is moderately rare. A solid shell; pinkish-white, with pale yellow bands on some specimens, and salmon-pink inside aperture; widely spaced coronations at shoulder. Average length 55 mm. See also Plate 31, No. 11.
13. **Conus kermadecensis** IREDALE. (= *C. fulmineus* Gmelin?) Dredged from 40 metres, Gulf of Papua. Range — Japan and Taiwan to Australia. An extremely variable species, it usually has a moderately tall spire, but odd specimens have the spire nearly flat. The figured specimen is typical of forms taken on offshore prawn grounds in southern Queensland and northern New South Wales. Average length 40 mm.
14. **Conus voluminalis** REEVE. Dredged 180 metres off Taiwan. Range unknown. Rare. A shiny shell of a light brown colour, with white bands at centre and shoulder, irregularly blotched and streaked with dark brown. Dark spiral lines encircle body whorl. Average length 45 mm.
15. **Conus pilkei** PETUCH.† New Britain. Range — Philippines and New Guinea to Fiji. Moderately rare. Variable in colour from off-white to yellow-brown, inside aperture bright orange; spire moderately tall, apex tinted brown; spaced deep grooves on base of body whorl, very fine close-set spiral lines above. Average length 50 mm.
16. **Conus suturatus** REEVE. South Queensland. Range — Indo-Pacific. A common species on east coast of Australia and New Guinea. A solid shell, extremely variable in colour ornamentation and form. Figured specimen closely resembles *C. tessulatus* in colour pattern, but has the typical sunken sutures and incised spiral lines between sutures, of *C. suturatus*. Average length 40 mm.
17. **Conus suturatus** REEVE. South Papuan coast. This form is the typical form with an inflated body whorl; depressed to flat spire, which contrasts strongly with previous specimen; white in colour, with bands of yellow, and a lavender tint at base. Occurs intertidal to several metres depth.
18. **Conus submarginatus** SOWERBY. New Caledonia. Range unknown. Rare. A glossy white shell, with brown tip to spire, and occasionally a cream to light brown tint at base; spire produced to sharp point, and comparatively smooth between sutures; very fine spiral lines on body whorl, slightly raised towards base. Figured specimen 44·45 mm.
19. **Conus pohlianus** SOWERBY. Rabaul, New Britain. Range — Philippines to New Guinea. Uncommon over most of its restricted range, but reasonably abundant in Rabaul area. Shell white, with two very pale broad cream bands, often not discernible, light brown near apex. Fresh specimens are cream inside aperture. Spire reasonably tall, with deep incised spiral lines between sutures; body whorl with widely spaced spiral grooves at base, and very fine lines above. Average length 65 mm.

† Usually labelled in collections as C. daullei Crosse. W. E. Old Jnr advises that *C. daullei* is the Madagascan representative of *C. magus*, and not the species illustrated here.

PLATE 34
1
2
3
4
5
6
7
8
9
10
11
12
13
14
15
16
17
18
19

FAMILY CONIDAE — continued.

1 to 3. Conus coronatus GMELIN. A series of specimens from the Papuan coast. An extremely variable species, common throughout the Indo-Pacific. *C. aristophanes* is recognized by some authorities, but complex intergradings make it difficult to justify this separation. A chubby shell, averaging 25 mm in length.

4 to 6. Conus miliaris HWASS. Manus Island, Admiralty Group. Indo-Pacific distribution. Common. An attractive little shell, not as solid as preceding species which it resembles. Average length 25 mm.

7. Conus miliaris HWASS. An unusual and attractive form from New Britain. Strongly pustulose over entire body whorl.

8 and 9. Conus fulgetrum SOWERBY. Ryukyu Islands. Indo-Pacific distribution. Uncommon. A close affinity to *C. miliaris* is obvious. Average length 25 mm.

10. Conus pauperculus SOWERBY. Appears restricted to southern Japan. Uncommon. A light brown shell, with a whitish band at centre; shoulder crenulated; spire with dark brown maculations. Average length 30 mm.

11. Conus moreleti CROSSE. Siassi Islands, west New Britain. Indo-Pacific range. Reasonably common. Easily recognized by the long slender body whorl and straight sides tapering to a narrow base. The shell is brown to purplish-brown, with pale blue-white bands at centre and shoulder; shoulder angulate and coronated; spire low and white in colour; base of shell purple; aperture very narrow. Average length 30 mm.

12 and 13. Conus ebraeus LINNE. Two colour forms from Port Moresby. A common Indo-Pacific species. A solid little cone; white to pink, usually with four rows of squarish black spots. Average length 30 mm.

14. Conus chaldaeus RÖDING. New Britain. Indo-Pacific range. Reasonably common. A white shell, odd specimens either pale yellow or pink, with vivid longitudinal streaks of black, broken by a narrow white band at centre of body whorl. Average length 25 mm.

15 and 16. Conus musicus HWASS. Port Moresby. Indo-Pacific range. Common. A small cone shell, white to blue-grey in colour, with rows of dark brown dots or dashes, irregular large blotches of brown or orange, and squarish black spots at shoulder. Average length 15 mm.

17 and 18. Conus sponsalis HWASS. Siassi Islands, west New Britain. Indo-Pacific range. A small solid shell with an inflated body whorl and low rounded spire; creamy white, with two rows of irregular brown blotches; base stained purple. Average length 20 mm.

19. Conus sponsalis HWASS. An unusual variety with raised spiral cords over entire body whorl.

20. Conus sponsalis HWASS (=*C. ceylanensis* HWASS). New Britain. A low spired unicoloured variety that appears to intergrade with the typical form.

21. Conus sponsalis HWASS (=*C. nanus* SOWERBY). Port Moresby. Appears to be between the typical *sponsalis* and the variety *ceylanensis*.

22. Conus sponsalis HWASS (=*C. nanus* SOWERBY). A uniform white shell from Rabaul, New Britain, with raised pustules over body whorl.

23. Conus cabritii BERNARDI. New Caledonia, to which area it is restricted. Uncommon. A small narrow, polished shell; coronated at shoulder; bluish-white in colour, with broad dark brown irregular streaks in a longitudinal pattern. Average length 15 mm.

24 and 25. Conus obscurus SOWERBY. Rabaul, New Britain. Indo-Pacific range. Uncommon. A smooth light-textured little shell, resembling a juvenile *C. geographus*. A piscivorous species capable of inflicting a painful sting. Coloration is variable, usually three rows of large irregular reddish-brown blotches on a pink or mauve background. Shoulder usually smooth, odd specimens with low crenulations or folds. Average length 30 mm.

26. Conus cyanostoma A. ADAMS. Queensland. Indo-Pacific range. Uncommon. Variable in colour from a uniform white to cream ornamented with irregular light brown zones. Body whorl has spaced spiral grooves. Average length 20 mm.

27 and 28. Conus papillosus KIENER. Samarai, eastern Papua. Indo-Pacific range. Uncommon. A most attractive little shell with a tall pointed spire; inflated body whorl, which is encircled with raised cords containing small reddish dots; base colour variable — blue-grey in specimens from Indonesia, yellow from Pacific Islands, and bright pink or yellow from New Guinea. Average length 15 mm.

29 and 30. Conus anemone LAMARCK. North-west Australia. A common species in the temperate waters of southern Australia, *C. anemone* ranges into the tropical Indo-Pacific along the north-west Australian coast in this form. Average length 30 mm.

31. Conus lienardi BERNARDI & CROSSE. Endemic to New Caledonia. Uncommon. A slender, highly polished shell, with a tall sharp spire; body whorl smooth, with spaced grooves; creamy-white in colour, densely ornamented with fine brown dots and streaks. Average length 40 mm.

32. Conus stramineus LAMARCK. Philippines. Central Indo-Pacific range. Reasonably common. A variable species, blue-grey in colour, variably marked with reddish-brown dots and spots; spire moderately tall and sharply pointed; spaced grooves over body whorl. Average length 40 mm.

33. Conus stramineus LAMARCK. Pacific Island form.

34. Conus stramineus LAMARCK (= *C. zebra* LAMARCK). Port Moresby. The Melanesian race of *C. stramineus*. A solid shell, with a lower spire than the northern race. The colour ornamentation tends to run in a longitudinal pattern. Occasionally dredged from 10 to 20 metres on the south Papuan coast.

35 and 36. Conus collisus REEVE. (=*C. subulatus* KIENER.) Philippines. Restricted to the Philippine Islands. Uncommon. A narrower shell than *C. stramineus*, it is deeply grooved at base of body whorl, smooth above. Average length 30 mm.

37. Conus andamanensis E. A. SMITH. Rabaul, New Britain. Central Indo-Pacific distribution. Rare in New Guinea waters. A highly polished shell ornamented with brown spots and zones; spire with six radiating brown lines; body whorl with widely spaced spiral grooves. Figured specimen 31·75 mm.

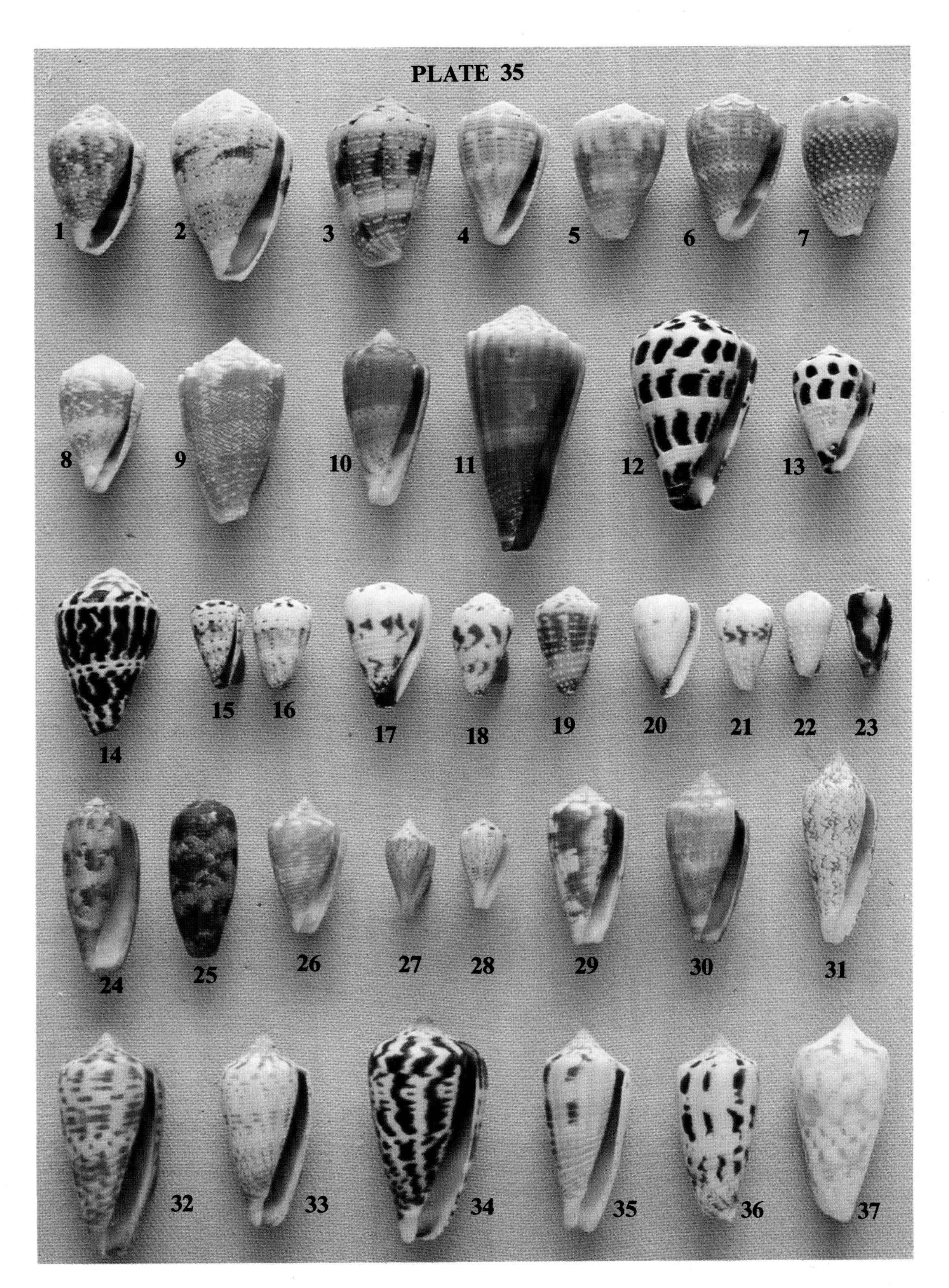
PLATE 35
1
2
3
4
5
6
7
8
9
10
11
12
13
14
15
16
17
18
19
20
21
22
23
24
25
26
27
28
29
30
31
32
33
34
35
36
37

FAMILY CONIDAE — continued.

1. Conus achatinus GMELIN. (=*monachus* LINNE?) Some collectors retain *C. achatinus* as a full species, but most taxonomists consider it only a form of *C. monachus*. The latter form lacks the spiral ridges and lines of *C. achatinus*. Range — Indo-Pacific, and reasonably common. This is a really beautiful species, with an amazing variation in colour pattern. Figured specimen is the typical form from north-west Australia. Grey-white, with two bands of irregular light brown blotches; spiral lines consisting of alternate brown and white spots and dashes. Operculum is small and narrow; periostracum reasonably thick, brown, and spirally tufted in young shells; smooth in aged specimens. Average length 45 mm.

2. Conus achatinus GMELIN. (=*monachus* LINNE?) Samarai form.

3. Conus achatinus GMELIN. (=*monachus* LINNE?) The figured specimen, with bold spiral lines, was dredged from 15 metres off Sepik River, New Guinea.

4. Conus achatinus GMELIN. (=*monachus* LINNE?) A dark purplish-black form with some blue-white zones, and heavy spiral lines. A lovely form from the south Papuan coast.

5. Conus achatinus GMELIN. (=*monachus* LINNE?) A broad heavy form from Malaya.

6. Conus monachus LINNE. Manus Island, Admiralty Group. Body whorl mainly smooth; some shallow grooves resticted to base. A brown and white nebulose pattern.

7. Conus monachus LINNE. Juvenile specimen from Rabaul, New Britain.

8. Conus catus HWASS. Rabaul, New Britain. An extremely variable species, which is abundant throughout the Indo-Pacific. Figured specimen is nearly black, with white blotches, upper part of body whorl smooth, lower half with beaded spiral ridges. Average length 40 mm.

9. Conus catus HWASS. This pale form from Siassi Islands, west New Britain, has smooth spiral ribs over entire body whorl.

10. Conus catus HWASS. An attractive pustulose form from Port Moresby.

11 to 13. Conus ranunculus HWASS. A common Indo-Pacific species. Until recently, this name had been applied to a Carribean species. The figured specimens were collected near Samarai, eastern Papua, and give some indication of the variable colour patterns of this species. A small solid shell, never attaining the size of *C. monachus* which it sometimes resembles. Average length 32 mm.

14 and 15. Conus thalassiarchus SOWERBY. Endemic to Philippine Islands where it is reasonably common. Variable, typical form has smooth, sharply angled shoulders; flattened spire with sharp apex; cream in colour, ornamented with fine brown dots in spiral rows; dark brown figurations forming bands; and base dark brown. Average length 75 mm.

16. Conus nodulosus SOWERBY. Restricted to west coast of Australia and uncommon. Cream in colour; ornamented with longitudinal wavy lines of light brown, leaving a pattern of small triangular areas, and two bands of brown blotches. Average length 40 mm.

17. Conus nobilis LINNE. An attractive and uncommon species with a restricted distribution centred about the Sulu Sea, Philippines. A golden-tan colour, variably ornamented with clear white spots arranged in bands. Average length 40 mm.

18. Conus sculletti MARSH. Dredged from 150-180 metres off east coast of Australia. Scarce. A slender cone, with flat spire and slightly concave sides and curving outer lip. White in colour, densely marked with tan-brown. Average length 40 mm.

19. Conus rufimaculosus MACPHERSON. Dredged 25-65 metres, east coast of Australia. Reasonably common. Spire depressed; pinkish-white, marked with rusty-brown; aperture pink to lilac. Average length 40 mm.

20. Conus furvus REEVE. Endemic to Philippine Islands, where it is reasonably common. A variable species, with many names applied to the varietal forms. A stout shell; straight sides; cream to fawn, variably marked with fine dark brown spiral lines, and two or more darker bands. Base purplish-brown. Average length 50 mm.

21. Conus circumactus IREDALE. Siassi Islands, west New Britain. Pacific Ocean range. An uncommon and attractive species. White, with pink to mauve zones, and variably marked with chestnut-brown blotches in two bands; fine spiral punctate grooves becoming postulose near base of shell. Aperture pinkish-white; lavender at base. Average length 45 mm.

22. Conus striatellus LINK. Port Moresby. Central Indo-Pacific range. Common. Similar to preceding species. A close relationship is evident. A white shell, ornamented with irregular large blotches of brown; aperture white; base of shell purplish-brown. Average length 50 mm.

23 and 24. Conus vitulinus HWASS. Port Moresby. Indo-Pacific range. Common. Distinguished by the depressed spire, sharp shoulder angle, and straight sides. Colour variable, usually white, attractively and variably ornamented with spiral lines of fine brown dots; two broad bands of dark brown; and broken longitudinal lines. Base purplish-brown. Average length 50 mm.

25. Conus planorbis BORN. Port Moresby. Indo-Pacific range. Common. A solid shell, very variable in colour and ornamentation. Usually a uniform cream to fawn, with a reddish-brown stain at base, and brown radiating lines on spire. Some forms are ornamented with a colour pattern closely resembling *C. vitulinus*, but can be readily distinguished by the heavier shell, and slightly convex rather than straight sides. Deepwater forms are usually paler and narrower. Average length 50 mm.

26. Conus planorbis BORN. (=*C. chenui* CROSS.) Yule Island, Gulf of Papua. A stout, patterned form, occurring rarely in New Guinea, Queensland and New Caledonia.

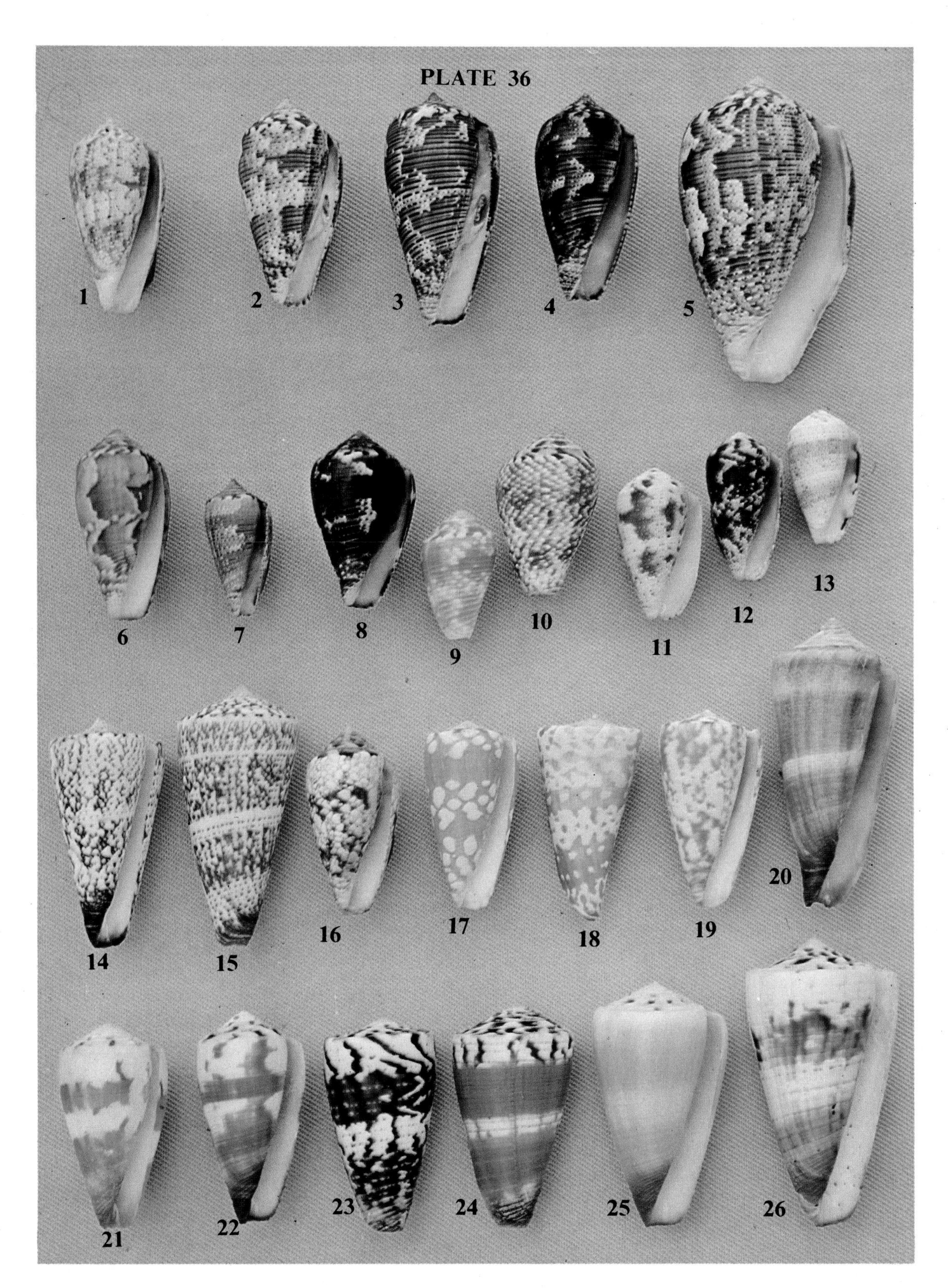
PLATE 36
1
2
3
4
5
6
7
8
9
10
11
12
13
14
15
16
17
18
19
20
21
22
23
24
25
26

FAMILY CONIDAE — continued.

This plate illustrates a group of cone shells usually referred to as the textiled cones. They are molluscivorous (feeding on other gastropod molluscs). In an aquarium, *C. textile* will kill and feed on *C. marmoreus*, another molluscivorous species. Large specimens of the common *C. textile* have caused human deaths. The textile cones have a wide aperture, a common characteristic in most forms of cone shells dangerous to man. This is an interesting fact and gives credence to the possibility that the potent efficiency of the venom apparatus of *C. textile* is, at least in part, a defensive mechanism. *C. marmoreus* is molluscivorous, but its venom is not as toxic to vertebrates. It has a comparatively narrow aperture. A wide flaring aperture offers less security to the mollusc, and aggression may be a retaliatory instinct. The piscivorous cones require a wide aperture to permit the intake of the victim (fish), which is swallowed whole, but it leaves the animal more vulnerable to other predators. Cones with wide apertures have been observed to be most aggressive and active after collection.

1 to 7. Conus textile LINNE. A series from New Guinea waters indicating the form and colour variation in this common species. It is widely distributed throughout the Indo-Pacific, with several names proposed for the more distinct variations. An attractive shell with its polished surface and dense colour ornamentation of white tent markings, spiral bands of brown, and longitudinal wavy streaks of dark brown. Average length 75 mm, with odd specimens attaining 125 mm.

8. Conus gloriamaris CHEMNITZ. The famous "glory of the seas" cone. The specimen illustrated was donated to the Port Moresby Museum by Mr Speer. It was collected in the Duke of York Islands which are situated between New Britain and New Ireland. Once a great rarity, this shell is now being recorded in reasonable numbers from the Rabaul area of New Britain, and in the Solomon Islands. In the Rabaul native market recently, three specimens were offered for sale on the one day, all at exorbitant prices. Supply is still much short of demand, and choice specimens bring about $250. Distribution is centred about western Melanesia, and it ranges from the islands of Indonesia and the Philippines to Fiji. Average length 100 mm. World record nearly 146 mm.

9 to 12. Conus canonicus HWASS **(tigrinus** SOWERBY**)**. A series from New Guinea. This species is quite distinct from *C. textile*. Its range appears restricted to the south-west Pacific, and is most abundant along northern coastline of New Guinea, and in the larger offshore islands. It lacks the longitudinal lines so consistent in *C. textile* and never attains the size of that species. A highly polished shell, usually with a bright pink aperture. Average length 40 mm.

13. Conus legatus LAMARCK. Manus Island, Admiralty Group. Indo-Pacific range. Moderately rare. A slender shell with rounded shoulder and tall pyramidal spire; beautifully coloured in pink to flesh, with fine network of light lines and odd large squarish blotches of dark reddish-brown; body whorl encircled by prominent corded ridges. A striking shell. Figured specimen 25 mm in length.

14 and 15. Conus retifer MENKE. Manus Island, Admiralty Group. Indo-Pacific range. Uncommon. A small, chubby, attractively ornamented shell, variable in colour pattern but remaining fairly consistent in form. White to pink, decorated with wavy longitudinal lines of orange-brown forming large whitish triangles, and two bands of darker brown; inside aperture often pink or lavender; deep spiral grooves on body whorl. Average length 32 mm.

PLATE 37
1
2
3
4
5
6
7
8
9
10
11
12
13
14
15

FAMILY CONIDAE — continued.

1. **Conus auratus** HWASS. New Ireland. Range — Pacific Ocean. A rare and beautiful species. A large slender shell, with a round sloping shoulder and moderately tall spire. Mid-tan in colour, with small pink tent marks in a longitudinal and nebulose pattern. The apparently unmarked areas, under magnification, are found to be ornamented with further minute tents arranged in spiral lines. Figured specimen 107·95 mm.

2. **Conus aulicus** LINNE. Siassi Islands, west New Britain. Indo-Pacific distribution. Uncommon. Proportionately broader than preceding species, with a shorter spire. A dark reddish-brown ground colour, ornamented with large pink-white triangular marks. Under magnification, the reddish-brown areas are lined with spiral ridges of a darker colour. Aperture creamy-yellow in fresh specimens. Average length 100 mm, but odd specimens attain 150 mm.

3. **Conus aulicus** LINNE. A colour variation from Samarai, eastern Papua, which is densely marked with smaller white triangular spots.

4. **Conus aureus** HWASS. Rabaul, New Britain. Indo-Pacific range. Moderately rare. A slender shell, with tall spire; prominent spiral ribs; coloured white with orange-brown longitudinal wavy lines and overlaying heavier streaks and blotches leaving a fine tent-like pattern. Specimens from Indian Ocean and from Philippines are more vividly marked. Average length 50 mm.

5 to 8. Conus omaria HWASS. Considered by many to be synonymous with *C. pennaceus* BORN, but most taxonomists and museum curators prefer to retain both names, claiming minor differences in shell characteristics, applying *C. pennaceus* to the Hawaiian representatives, and *C. omaria* for the central Indo-Pacific forms. There is uncertainty as to where the Red Sea and some African forms fit into this pattern. A common species, it has a low, rounded spire, with nipple-like apical point. The specimens figured here were collected in the one locality, near Samarai, eastern Papua, indicating the diversity of form and colour of this species. No. 7 may be regarded as a typical form; No. 6, paler than normal; and Nos. 5 and 8 have a melanistic tendency. Average length 60 mm.

9 to 12. Conus episcopus HWASS. Port Moresby. Indo-Pacific range. Reasonably common. Figured specimens are a growth series from the one locality, illustrating the changing pattern of the growing shells. Juveniles are decorated with alternating longitudinal wavy broad bands of brown and white; developing with maturity into a scattered tent pattern. Aged specimens closely resemble *C. omaria*, but young shells are readily distinguishable.
C. episcopus is a narrower shell and with a more produced spire than *C. omaria*, and is generally more solid. Average length 65 mm.

13. Conus nimbosus HWASS. Wewak, New Guinea, which is probably an extension to the previously known range of this rare species, which has previously been reported from northern shores of the Indian Ocean from Malaya to East Africa. Figured specimen is 42 mm in length.

PLATE 38
1
2
3
4
5
6
7
8
9
10
11
12
13

FAMILY CONIDAE — continued.

It is little wonder that cone shells are so popular with collectors when you study the eye-pleasing form and the striking colour ornamentation of the shells illustrated on this plate. The "rich" and the "poor" appear here together — *C. crocatus* is a great rarity; its true value is unknown as it seldom changes hands. On the other hand, *C. generalis*, as beautiful as its colouring may be, is a common species.

1. **Conus crocatus** LAMARCK. Samarai, eastern Papua. Range — western Pacific. Very rare. A smooth, polished shell, with rounded shoulder and moderately tall and sharp spire, Colouring is saffron-brown, stained darker at base, sparsely and irregularly decorated with odd shaped white spots which appear also on the spire. The porcelaineous aperture contrasts with the body colour. The body whorl is encircled with fine rounded ridges which become obsolete on upper part. Figured specimen 63·5 mm in length.

2. **Conus circumcisus** BORN. (=*C. brazieri* SOWERBY.) Louisiade Archipelago, eastern Papua. Central Indo-Pacific range. A rare species that appears to have its centre of distribution in New Britain. A solid shell, consistent in form, but extremely variable in colour, hence the synonymy and confusion regarding this shell. Usually mauve to pale lavender in live specimens, with two or three brown bands and sparsely spotted with dark brown to black; spiral ridges on body whorl are coloured, forming brown lines, sometimes broken into spots or dashes; spire marked with whitish blotches. Average length 76 mm.

3 and 4. Conus magnificus REEVE. Samarai, eastern Papua. Distribution appears restricted to the islands of Melanesia in the south-west Pacific, and is uncommon. Mr W. E. Old of The American Museum of Natural History examined these specimens and advised (*in litteris*) that they match Reeve's original description and figure of the species. Its closest relative is *C. episcopis* in form and colour pattern. A shell from the Red Sea area is appearing in collections as *C. magnificus*, but these are of the *omaria-pennaceus* complex. *C. magnificus* is a really beautiful shell, and aptly named. It is highly polished, with fine spiral ridges at base of body whorl; shoulder is rounded, and it has a moderately produced but rounded spire; reddish-brown in colour, with longitudinally arranged cloudy patches of large and minute pink tent-like spots; aperture white, sometimes creamy-yellow deep within. Average length 60 mm.

5 and 6. Conus telatus REEVE. Philippines. Appears endemic to the Philippine Islands. Uncommon. A slender and graceful shell with a colour pattern similar to *C. textile*, but is coronated at shoulder and on spire, and the body whorl is encircled with prominent corded ridges. An attractive and distinctive shell. Average length 65 mm.

7. **Conus ammiralis** LINNE. Dredged off Sepik River, north coast of New Guinea. Indo-Pacific range. Uncommon. The high polish of this really lovely shell rivals that of the cowries and olives. It is a white shell with such elaborate and complex ornamentation that no description could adequately describe the pattern which varies in fine detail from shell to shell. *C. architalassus*, which is coronated, is a rare deepwater form of *C. ammiralis*. Average length 76 mm.

8 to 10. Conus generalis LINNE. A series of colour variants from New Guinea. Indo-Pacific range. Common. Very variable in colour and ornamentation as shown by specimens figured, but is consistent in form. A graceful shell, with sharply angled shoulder and concave spire with an unusually produced apex, often eroded in aged specimens. The sides are straight to slightly concave in some forms, tapering to a narrow base. The body whorl is smooth and highly polished. Average length 70 mm.

11. **Conus litoglyphus** HWASS. Siassi Islands, west New Britain. Indo-Pacific range. Reasonably common. Lacks the high polish of previous species, but the contrasting white markings on the reddish-brown base colour attract attention. Average length 50 mm.

12. **Conus litoglyphus** HWASS. A low spired, less brilliantly marked form from Port Moresby.

PLATE 39
1
2
3
4
5
6
7
8
9
10
11
12

FAMILY CONIDAE — continued.

1 and 2. Conus nussatella LINNE. Manus Island, Admiralty Group. Indo-Pacific range. Uncommon. A narrow, solid shell; spiral grooves crossed by fine axial ridges; colour white, ornamented with rows of brown dots and some irregular blotches. Average length 50 mm.

3. Conus tenellus DILLWYN. Samarai, eastern Papua. Range — central Indo-Pacific. Rare. Slender; with prominent spiral grooves and axial ribs; light brown, with cream blotches and pink to mauve cloudy zones. Average length 40 mm.

4 and 5. Conus terebra BORN. Port Moresby. Indo-Pacific range. Reasonably common. Covered in life with a thick brown velvety periostracum. A solid shell; body whorl encircled with raised spiral ridges; shape variable as indicated in illustrations; colour white to bluish-grey, with two or more broad bands of either yellow or mauve; stained purple at base. Average length 65 mm.

6. Conus species, possibly *C. violaceus* SOWERBY. W. E. Old Jnr. suggested this name with reservation, as the name *violaceus* had been proposed previously by the authors Gmelin, Link, and Reeve. An uncommon species which appears restricted to north Australia. Average length 50 mm.

7. Conus auricomus HWASS. New Britain. Indo-Pacific range. Uncommon. A slender attractive shell; spire rounded; fine spiral ridges on body whorl; ornamented with a tented pattern and two bands of brown. Average length 45 mm.

8. Conus glans HWASS. Port Moresby. Indo-Pacific range. Uncommon. Small and rather solid; body whorl with corded spiral ridges; coloured purple, with lighter band at centre; apex with pink apical tip; aperture purple. Average length 25 mm.

9 and 10. Conus scabriusculus DILLWYN. Port Moresby. Western Pacific range. Uncommon. A small solid shell; granular spiral ridges; purplish-brown in colour, with large white patches; spire mostly white, with sharp pink apex. Average length 30 mm.

11. Conus luteus BRODERIP. Rabaul, New Britain. Indo-Pacific range. Rare. A small smooth shell; spire rounded and produced; a deep yellow colour, ornamented with rows of fine brown dots, a light brown band at centre, and a row of orange-brown squarish spots. Figured specimen 25 mm in length.

12 and 13. Conus mitratus HWASS. Samarai, eastern Papua. Indo-Pacific distribution. Moderately rare. As the name implies, this species resembles the mitres in general shape. Cream to yellow in colour, ornamented below shoulder with two rows of dark brown blotches and longitudinal streaks, above the shoulder angle decorated with squarish brown spots. Average length 25 mm.

14. Conus cylindraceus BRODERIP & SOWERBY. Samarai, eastern Papua. Indo-Pacific range. Moderately rare. A slender, smooth and highly polished shell; honey-brown in colour, marked with irregular longitudinal streaks and patches of white. Figured specimen 25 mm.

15 and 16. Conus pertusus HWASS. Louisiade Archipelago, eastern Papua. Indo-Pacific range. Moderately rare. If this species were a little larger, it could be described as one of the most beautiful of all the cones. Even so, the colours are startling. A thin-textured shell, with a frail lip; red in colour, with rows of pinkish-white clouded blotches at shoulder, centre and base; aperture mauve to lavender. The body whorl is comparatively smooth and highly polished, ridged towards base. Average length 32 mm.

17 and 18. Conus floridulus ADAMS & REEVE. Dredged 37 metres, Gulf of Papua. Further specimens have recently been dredged from similar depth near Samarai, eastern Papua. Range unknown, but probably restricted to south-west Pacific. Rare. An attractive species with stepped and sharply pointed spire; straight sides; sharply angled shoulder; colour variable, usually white, with irregular brown markings; base and aperture lilac. Average length 40 mm.

19. Conus floridulus ADAMS & REEVE. An unusual and beautiful form with coronated shoulder and rows of pustules over the entire body whorl. Dredged from 40 metres off Yule Island, Papua.

20. Conus coccineus GMELIN. Samarai, Papua. Distribution — south-west Pacific. Moderately rare. A strikingly attractive shell; shoulder crenulated in adult specimens; sculptured with granular spiral ridges; coloured orange-red, with a white band which is decorated with dark brown spots and blotches. Average length 32 mm.

21 and 22. Conus aureolus SOWERBY. Samarai, Papua. Range unknown. Rare. A small frail, smooth and highly polished shell, with angulate shoulder; concave spire produced to a sharp apex; sides straight; narrow at base; colour varies from yellow to pink and brown, with white band at centre and brown blotches on spire. Average length 25 mm.

23 and 24. Conus varius LINNE. Port Moresby. Indo-Pacific range. Uncommon. A solid coronated shell, with granulated spiral ridges and moderately tall spire; variable in shape as illustrations show, but readily distinguishable. White in colour, with brown band below centre and a row of large blotches below shoulder, and an overall sprinkling of fine dots. Average length 45 mm.

25. Conus generalis LINNE. A dwarf form from Goodenough Island, eastern Papua, where the population of this species averages 38 mm. See also Plate 39.

26. Conus timorensis HWASS. Tagula Island, eastern Papua. Distribution — central Indo-Pacific. Rare. Figured specimen is a dead shell, but gives some indication of the delicate colouring of this species. Figured specimen 44·45 mm.

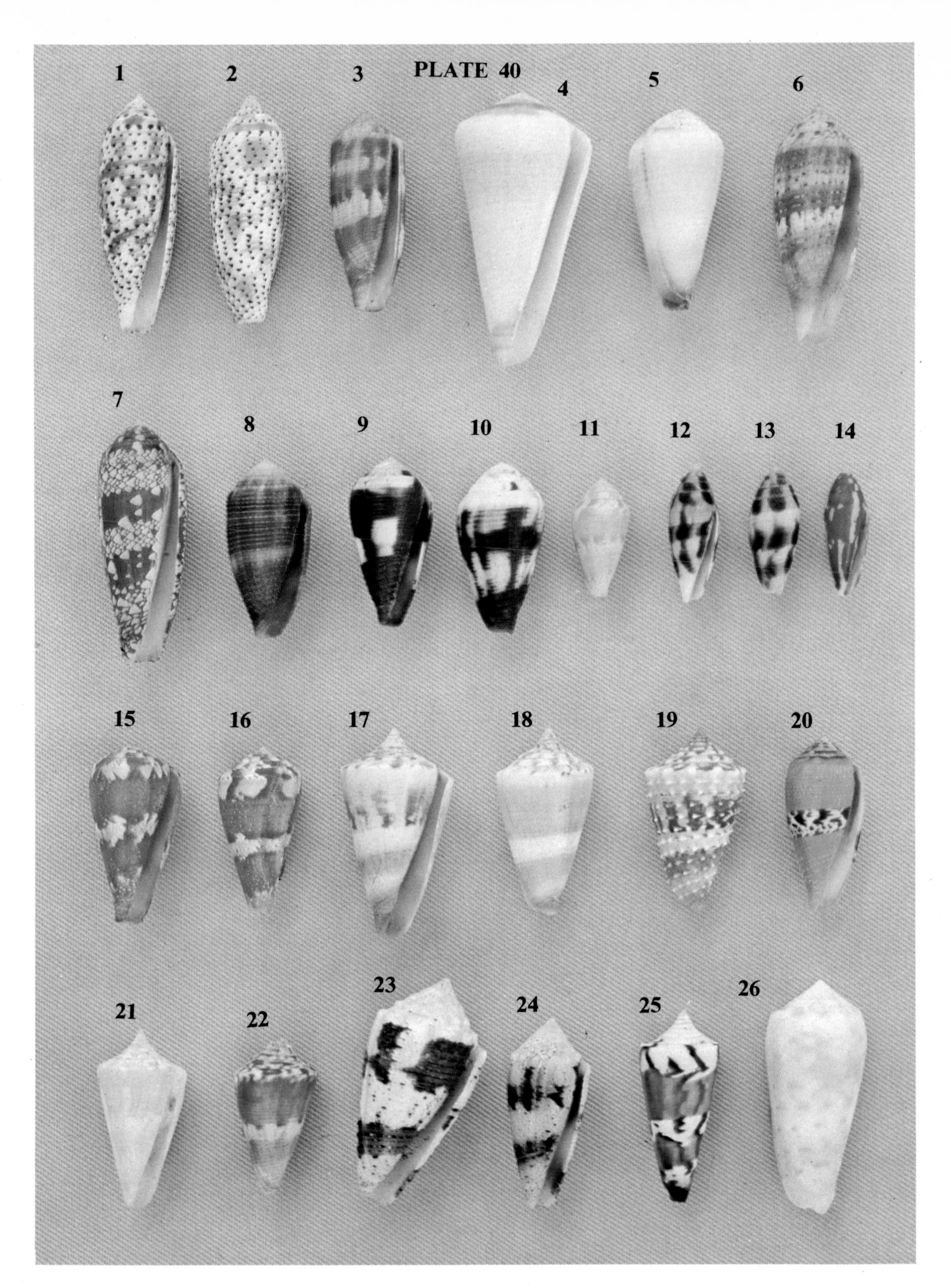
PLATE 40
1
2
3
4
5
6
7
8
9
10
11
12
13
14
15
16
17
18
19
20
21
22
23
24
25
26

FAMILY CONIDAE — continued.

1. **Conus striatus** LINNE. Port Moresby. Indo-Pacific range. Common. A large, solid, and attractive shell. One of the known dangerous species. Body whorl finely but deeply striated; spire channelled between sutures; aperture moderately wide; colour variable, usually pinkish, with irregular brown figurations. Average length 75 mm.
2. **Conus striatus** LINNE. A dark variety from Siassi Islands, west New Britain.
3. **Conus striatus** LINNE. An unusual colour form from Rabaul, New Britain. The molluscan fauna of this volcanic island includes many deviations from the normal form.
4. **Conus striatus** LINNE. Figured specimen, devoid of the usual colour and ornamentation, was collected alive with the previous specimen. Another example of the colour variation in Conus species, even in the one population.
5. **Conus floccatus** SOWERBY. A rare species, restricted to the western Pacific, with centre of distribution in the Marshall Islands. A solid, attractive shell; pinkish-white, with spiral rows of brown spots, and larger blotches. Average length 55 mm.
6. **Conus suratensis** HWASS. Dredged from 15 metres off Sepik River, New Guinea. Restricted to the tropical seas of the central Indo-Pacific. Not common. Similar to *C. betulinus*, it is probably an offshore relative of this species, though it is consistently smaller, and of frailer structure. An orange-fawn shell, ornamented with spiral rows of brown dots appearing in longitudinal lines. Average length 55 mm.
7. **Conus betulinus** LINNE. Intertidal on sand and grass, Bogia, New Guinea. Indo-Pacific distribution. Reasonably common. A solid, heavy shell, averaging 100 mm, but odd specimens attain 180 mm. Yellow in colour, with white spiral bands decorated with black dots and dashes in a most attractive pattern. Spire with radiating black lines.
8. **Conus glaucus** LINNE. Madang, New Guinea. Distribution restricted to the west Pacific. Not common. A slate-grey colour, decorated with spiral rows of black and white dashes; spire with broad radiating black lines. Average length 40 mm.
9. **Conus glaucus** LINNE. Specimen with periostracum intact.
10. **Conus figulinus** LINNE. 9 metres, Gulf of Papua. Indo-Pacific range. A common species from intertidal sand flats to about 20 metres depth. Variable; light to dark brown, with darker spiral lines. Average length 65 mm.
11. **Conus quercinus** SOLANDER. Port Moresby. Indo-Pacific range. A common sand-dwelling species from low tide level to several metres depth. A solid shell; yellow in colour, with very fine spiral lines of brown. Average length 65 mm.
12. **Conus concolor** SOWERBY. Moturina Island, Louisiade Archipelago, eastern Papua. Appears restricted to the south-west Pacific, with distribution centred about the New Guinea Islands. A rare shell. Uniform tan-brown; polished; body whorl smooth, except for a few spiral grooves at base, and weak axial growth lines. Average length 45 mm.
13. **Conus concolor** SOLANDER. A dark brown specimen from Bougainville Island.
14. **Conus cinereus** HWASS. Philippines. Distribution — central Indo-Pacific. Reasonably common. A slender shell with a sharp tapering spire. An extremely variable species, with many named varietal forms. The figured specimen is a dark blue-grey, attractively marked with faint brown and white dots in spiral rows between a series of deep grooves; with some larger markings. Average length 50 mm.
15. **Conus cinereus** HWASS. A colour variant from south coast of New Britain Island.

PLATE 41
1
2
3
4
5
6
7
8
9
10
11
12
13
14
15

FAMILY CONIDAE — continued.

1. Conus malaccanus HWASS. Tagula Island, Louisiade Archipelago, eastern Papua. Restricted to central Indo-Pacific. Moderately rare. A white shell; attractively ornamented with two bands of brown joined by longitudinal streaks. Figured specimen 64 mm in length.

2. Conus vexillum GMELIN. Port Moresby. Indo-Pacific range. Reasonably common. A large, lightweight shell, often disfigured with healed scars. Brown in colour, with broken white band at centre, repeated in some specimens at shoulder; spire decorated with large white and brown blotches; base purplish-brown; interior white. The operculum is narrow and long, usually about one-third length of aperture. Average length 90 mm.

3. Conus vexillum GMELIN. Juvenile specimen.

4 and 5. Conus capitaneus LINNE. Yule Island, Papua. Indo-Pacific range. Common. A variable species, usually olive to light brown, ornamented with white bands at centre and shoulder; the white zones further decorated with one or two rows of irregular black spots; body whorl encircled with spiral lines or dots; spire with large brown and white blotches. The operculum is very large, occupying two fifths of aperture. Average length 65 mm.

6. Conus trigonus REEVE. Restricted to north-west Australia. Uncommon. Similar in form to preceding species. Spire low, sometimes flat; shell thin; light brown to tan in colour, with darker spiral lines; a broad broken white band at centre, and a narrower band at shoulder; spire with brown and white radiating streaks. Average length 65 mm.

7. Conus mustelinus HWASS. Port Moresby. Indo-Pacific range. Uncommon. Narrower, and with taller spire than preceding species with which it is often confused. Usually yellow-brown; white band at centre, decorated with two or three rows of black spots; narrow band at shoulder with dark brown streaks; spire with large dark brown and white squarish blotches. Operculum about one third length of aperture. Average length 75 mm.

8 and 9. Conus miles LINNE. Port Moresby. Indo-Pacific range. Very common. A creamy-white shell, attractively ornamented with thin, wavy, light brown longitudinal lines, and some broader streaks; two spiral bands of dark brown; purplish-brown zone covering lower portion of body whorl. Average length 65 mm.

10 and 11. Conus rattus HWASS. Port Moresby. Indo-Pacific range. Very common species. A small dark brown shell; ornamented with a row of white blotches at shoulder; an obsolete band at centre of body whorl; sprinkled overall with small to minute bluish-white spots. Average length 30 mm.

12 and 13. Conus geographus LINNE. New Britain Island. Indo-Pacific range. Reasonably common. Several deaths have been recorded following unjuries inflicted by the Geography Cone. A large, attractive shell, surprisingly frail for its size; with a wide aperture and thin lip; short spire; coronated shoulder; coloured creamy-white, and blotched, freckled and spotted with reddish-brown. Average length 100 mm.

14 and 15. Conus tulipa LINNE. Trobriand Islands. Central Indo-Pacific range. Uncommon. A piscivorous species, dangerous to man. A light-weight shell; slightly coronated; large, wide aperture and thin outer lip; beautifully marked with shades of pink, bluish-white and red-brown, in a longitudinal nebulose pattern; encircled overall with spiral rows of brown and white dots. Average length 55 mm.

PLATE 42
1
2
3
4
5
6
7
8
9
10
11
12
13
14
15

FAMILY CONIDAE — continued.

1. Conus magus LINNE. Porebada, near Port Moresby. Indo-Pacific range. A pale form with some pink zones and two broad pale brown bands and fine dark dots in spiral rows; spire low and blotched with brown. Figured specimen 44.45 mm.

2 to 4. Conus magus LINNE. Colour variants from Port Moresby. Indo-Pacific range. Common. A piscivorous species and highly venomous, though no instances of injuries have been reported. The aperture is not as wide as in other fish-eating species, and the shell is solid. The animal appears content to retract into its shell for protection, for it is a timid creature in captivity. Extremely variable in shape and colour. Average length 50 mm.

5. Conus magus LINNE. A heavy form with greatly inflated body whorl, and nearly flat spire, from Sabah Island, north Borneo. Average length 55 mm.

6. Conus magus LINNE. A handsome specimen from Palawan Island. Often referred to as the "golden" or "orange" *magus*.

7. Conus epistomioides WEINKAUFF. Port Moresby. A narrow, smooth and highly polished shell, with a frail lip; variable in colour pattern, but always attractively marked. A piscivorous species. Dr A. J. Kohn considers this shell to be another variant of *C. magus*.

8. Conus epistomioides WEINKAUFF. Colour form from Samarai, eastern Papua.

9. Conus lynceus SOWERBY. Dredged 37 metres, south Papuan coast. Indo-Pacific range. Uncommon offshore. A lightweight shell; attractive in form and ornamentation; has a tall pointed spire; gracefully tapering body whorl which is polished, and encircled with spaced spiral grooves; cream in colour, profusely decorated with small to medium sized squarish brown spots and some larger irregular blotches. Average length 60 mm.

10 to 12. Conus lividus HWASS. Colour variants from south Papuan coast. Indo-Pacific range. Abundant. Extremely variable in colour, with several names proposed for colour forms. Ranges in colour from light yellow-fawn to dark purplish-brown, with whitish bands at centre and shoulder; spire white in lighter coloured forms, but stained with the shade of the body whorl in darker specimens; coronated; aperture narrow; base of shell purplish-brown. Average length 40 mm.

13 and 14. Conus frigidus REEVE. Siassi Islands, west New Britain. Indo-Pacific range. Common. Juvenile shells are white, adults yellow-brown to olive; aperture, base, and apex purple; spire low and rounded; body whorl corded near base. Averages 32 mm.

15 and 16. Conus balteatus SOWERBY. Siassi Islands, west New Britain. Indo-Pacific range. Reasonably common. Variable in colour from light olive-fawn to dark brown, with irregular whitish blotches tending to form bands at centre and shoulder, and flecked over-all with blue-white dots; spire white, with a pink apex; shoulder coronated; body whorl prominently striated. Averages 40 mm.

17 and 18. Conus sugillatus REEVE. (= *C. muriculatus* SOWERBY.) Port Moresby. Indo-Pacific range. Examination of a large number of shells shows that this common intertidal species intergrades with the deep-water *muriculatus*. Usually smooth, but in a series, some have the spiral ridges becoming prominent and corded, and even postulose in odd specimens. Average length 40 mm.

19. Conus muriculatus SOWERBY. Dredged 27 metres, Port Moresby. A moderately rare form from deeper water. Has a distinct colour pattern, and spaced rows of spinose ridges. Most attractive. Average length 25 mm.

20. Conus cumingi REEVE (1848). Figured specimen of 28·5 mm was collected by Roger Buick on Hisiu beach near Port Moresby. Other specimens have recently been found by snorkel divers off Yule Island in the Gulf of Papua.

21. Conus moluccensis KUSTER. Samarai, Papua. Central Indo-Pacific range. Rare. A cream shell, with broken lines of brown on corded spiral ridges, and two rows of large blotches; spire coronated and produced to a fine apex. Averages 40 mm.

22. Conus moluccensis KUSTER. A heavier and wider form, with dark coloration, from 15 metres off Sepik River, New Guinea. Figured specimen 44·45 mm.

23. Conus moluccensis KUSTER. A small, narrow form with very prominent raised spiral ridges of dark brown to black, and a low spire. Figured specimen 25·4 mm.

24. Conus boeticus REEVE. New Britain. Range, Indonesia and New Guinea to Fiji. Uncommon. A highly polished shell, creamy-white in colour, ornamented with large irregular blotches of dark brown, leaving broken bands at shoulder, centre and base; low rounded nodules at shoulder; spire sharp and tipped with pink; raised spiral cords at base of body whorl, smooth above. Average length 25 mm.

25. Conus species. Possibly a small form and variant of *C. comatosa* PILSBRY. Dredged 37 metres, Gulf of Papua. A slender graceful little cone shell, with its wide and sharply angled shoulder, tall pointed spire, and slightly concave sides tapering to a very narrow base. It is bluish-white in colour, with variable bandings, and is spotted on spire with dark brown. Figured specimen 28·57 mm. See also Plate 44, No. 12.

26. Conus semisulcatus SOWERBY. Rabaul, New Britain. Uncommon. Has wide, sharply angled shoulders; tall spotted spire with sharp apex; body whorl deeply grooved on lower half, smooth and polished above; white in colour, with pale pink tonings, a white and two broken brown bands at centre; spire with brown blotches; base pale lilac. Figured specimen 25·4 mm.

27. Conus species. W. R. Old Jnr. suggests this cone is possibly *C. anabathrum* CROSSE. Dredged by Tom Nielsen from 48 metres off central Queensland coast. An attractive species, with a tall stepped spire; body whorl highly polished; regular spaced spiral grooves; coloured orange-brown, lilac towards base, a whitish band at centre bordered by a row of brown spots; apex white with brown maculations. Figured specimen 25·4 mm.

PLATE 43

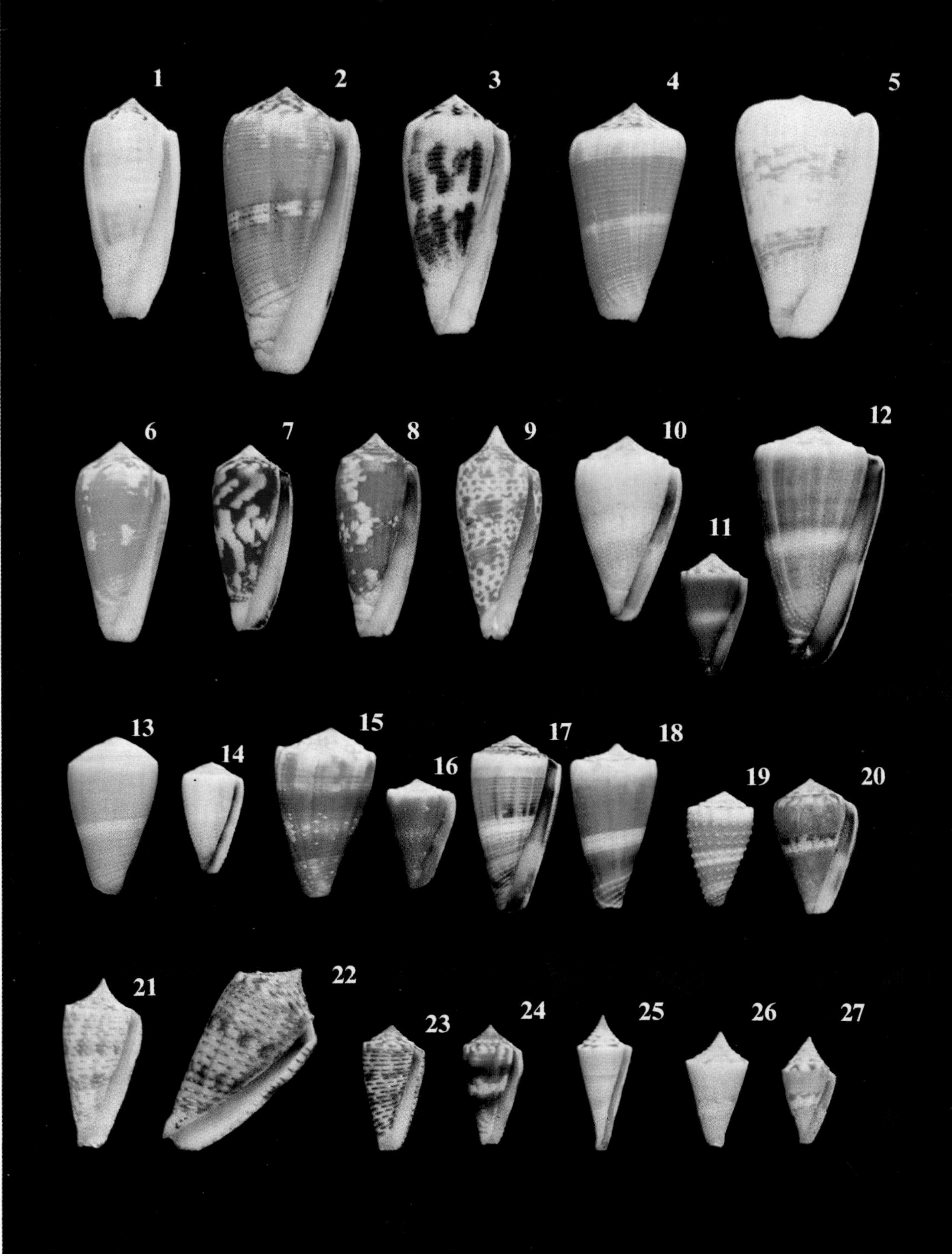

FAMILY CONIDAE — continued.

1. Conus australis HOLTEN. Taiwan. Appears restricted to China Sea. Reasonably common. A large solid shell, with a tall spire and coarse surface formed by heavily corded ridges on the body whorl. White to cream in colour, densely ornamented with brown dots, streaks, and irregular larger blotches in three or four bands. Average length 90 mm.

2. Conus sulcatus HWASS. China Sea. Range, central Indo-Pacific. Reasonably common. A solid shell; crenulated at shoulder; spire low, with produced nipple-like apex; whorl with widely spaced, deep, smooth grooves; colour off-white to cream-fawn, spire white. Average length 65 mm.

3 and 4. Conus sulcatus HWASS. Rabaul, New Britain. This form has more prominent nodules at shoulder, the grooves are more numerous and beaded on the raised ridges. Fig. 4 is a juvenile shell which will lose the brown colour and smooth surface with development. A series shows the intergrading growth stages. This form attains 76 mm in New Britain.

5. Conus grangeri SOWERBY. Philippines. Distribution uncertain. Comparatively rare. Awhite shell, with brown dashes and spots arranged in bands; intricately sculptured with alternating broad rounded ridges, and narrow beaded ridges. A striking shell. Figured specimen 50 mm.

6. Conus pseudosulcatus NOMURA. The type specimen is a Japanese fossil shell, but has recently been taken alive from deep water in the China Sea. Figured specimen dredged south-west of Taiwan. Uncommon. A white shell, with fawn zones; the tall spire is marked with brown streaks. Sculpturing varies from comparatively smooth spiral ribs to prominent pustulose ridges. Average length 40 mm.

7. Conus alabaster REEVE. Philippines. Range unknown. Uncommon. A white shell decorated with brown blotches and streaks which become dense on spire; sculptured with widely spaced spiral cords. Average length 40 mm.

8 and 9. Conus mucronatus REEVE. Rabaul, New Britain. Although the type locality is Philippines, this shell appears endemic to the New Britain area, where it is common in beach-washed debris, but scarce in live condition. A white shell, with brown spiral ridges encircling the body whorl, and the spire with radiating brown lines. The density of the colouring varies, but the shape is constant. Average length 40 mm.

10. Conus orbignyi AUDOUIN. Dredged off Taiwan. Range, China Sea. Reasonably common offshore. A beautiful shell, with a long tapering body whorl and tall spire, stepped and roundly coronated. The surface is deeply grooved, and densely spotted in reddish-brown, and rows of larger markings. The lip is gracefully curved. Averages 65 mm.

11. Conus ichinoseana KURODA. Restricted to deep water off southern Japan. Moderately rare. A glossy shell, grooved on lower part of whorl, smooth above; spire tall, stepped and crenulated above sutures; white in colour, variably marked with dots and streaks of brown. Averages 65 mm.

12. Conus comatosa PILSBRY. This large form appears restricted to the deep waters of southern Japan. A rare and attractive species, with a long slender whorl tapering to an extremely fine base; stepped spire; whorl sculptured with smooth grooves, and ornamented with four rows of broken brown bands and small dots. Figured specimen 50·8 mm. See also Plate 43, No. 25.

13. Conus cancellatus HWASS. Japan. Range, Japan to Philippines. Uncommon. Has a tall stepped spire, and deeply grooved body whorl; coloured white, and marked on spire and upper part of whorl with irregular and variable brown blotches. Average length 40 mm.

14. Conus praecellens A. ADAMS. Japan. Range, Japan to South-east Asia. Uncommon. The spire is stepped; shoulder with low granules; the long body whorl is finely grooved; white, with brown dots on the spiral ridges, and larger blotches in two bands. Average length 32 mm.

15. Conus sowerbii REEVE. Philippines. Range from South-east Asia to New Guinea. Moderately rare. Distinguished by its unusually tall spire; sharply angled and smooth shoulder; and deep spiral grooves. A cream shell, with reddish-brown spots on the ridges, and three rows of larger blotches. Figured specimen 32 mm.

16. Conus sowerbii REEVE. Rabaul, New Britain. Has a more inflated body whorl than the Philippine form, and the more numerous ridges are corded. Figured specimen 32 mm.

17. Conus acutangulus LAMARCK. Port Moresby. Appears in isolated populations in deep water throughout the central Indo-Pacific, but not common anywhere. Often confused with *C. sowerbii*, but can be distinguished by the comparatively straight lines of the spire and whorl; deep punctate grooves; and beaded spire. Average length 25 mm.

18. Conus species (possibly *wakayamaensis* KURODA). Japan. Endemic to south Japan. Rare in live condition, dead specimens taken in coral dredges. Has low spire and straight sides; is lightly grooved; white in colour, with brown blotches arranged in two or three rows. Figured specimen 25·4 mm.

19. Conus vimineus REEVE. Philippines. Appears endemic to the Philippine Islands. Uncommon. A slender shell, with a long body whorl; close-set punctate grooves; medium spire with straight sides; fawn to light brown in colour, with indistinct rows of squarish blotches. Averages 32 mm.

20. Conus insculptus KIENER. Dredged 37 metres, Gulf of Papua. Range unknown. Rarely collected alive. The acute shoulder angle, long tapering whorl, and tall stepped and beaded spire, are distinctive. The surface is smoothly grooved, white in colour, with irregular bands of light brown. Figured specimen 25·4 mm.

21. Conus aculeiformis REEVE. Dredged 40 metres, Port Moresby. Range uncertain. Rare. An extremely slender shell, with a tall spire and sharp apex; a long whorl with straight sides tapering to a fine base; deep grooves separated by wide, flat and polished ridges; decorated with small squarish brown spots and two rows of larger blotches. Figured specimen 28·57 mm.

22. Conus aculeiformis REEVE. Colour form from Rabaul, New Britain.

23. Conus eximius REEVE. Malaya. Range, South-east Asia. Rare. A smooth shell, highly polished, with widely spaced grooves on lower part of body whorl, smooth above; shoulder smooth and sharply angled; spire low but produced to a sharp apex; white in colour, with irregular orange-brown blotches and streaks arranged in two broad bands. Figured specimen 25·4 mm.

24. Conus capitanellus FULTON. Endemic to off-shore waters in southern Japan. Uncommon. Shoulder is smooth and sharply angled; the spire is low, rounded, with a fine apical point; sides are straight; whorl smooth and polished; honey-brown in colour, with three rows of white longitudinal blotches which continue on to spire. Average length 32 mm.

25. Conus kimioi HABE. Dredged from 180 metres, south Japan. Range unknown. Very rare. An unmistakable species, with its sharply angled shoulder, low rounded spire, long body whorl, and unusually sharp base. Figured specimen 19·05 mm.

26. Conus urashimanus KURODA & ITO. Dredged 180 metres, Taiwan. Distribution, central Indo-Pacific. Moderately rare. The figured specimen is an attractive young shell which is a soft lilac in colour, with two indistinct bands of brown blotches, and smooth and polished. Aged specimens are whitish to pale grey, and sometimes corded near base. The spire is low, rounded, with a fine apex. Figured specimen is 38·1 mm, but it attains 76 mm.

PLATE 44
1
2
3
4
5
6
7
8
9
10
11
12
13
14
15
16
17
18
19
20
21
22
23
24
25
26

Index

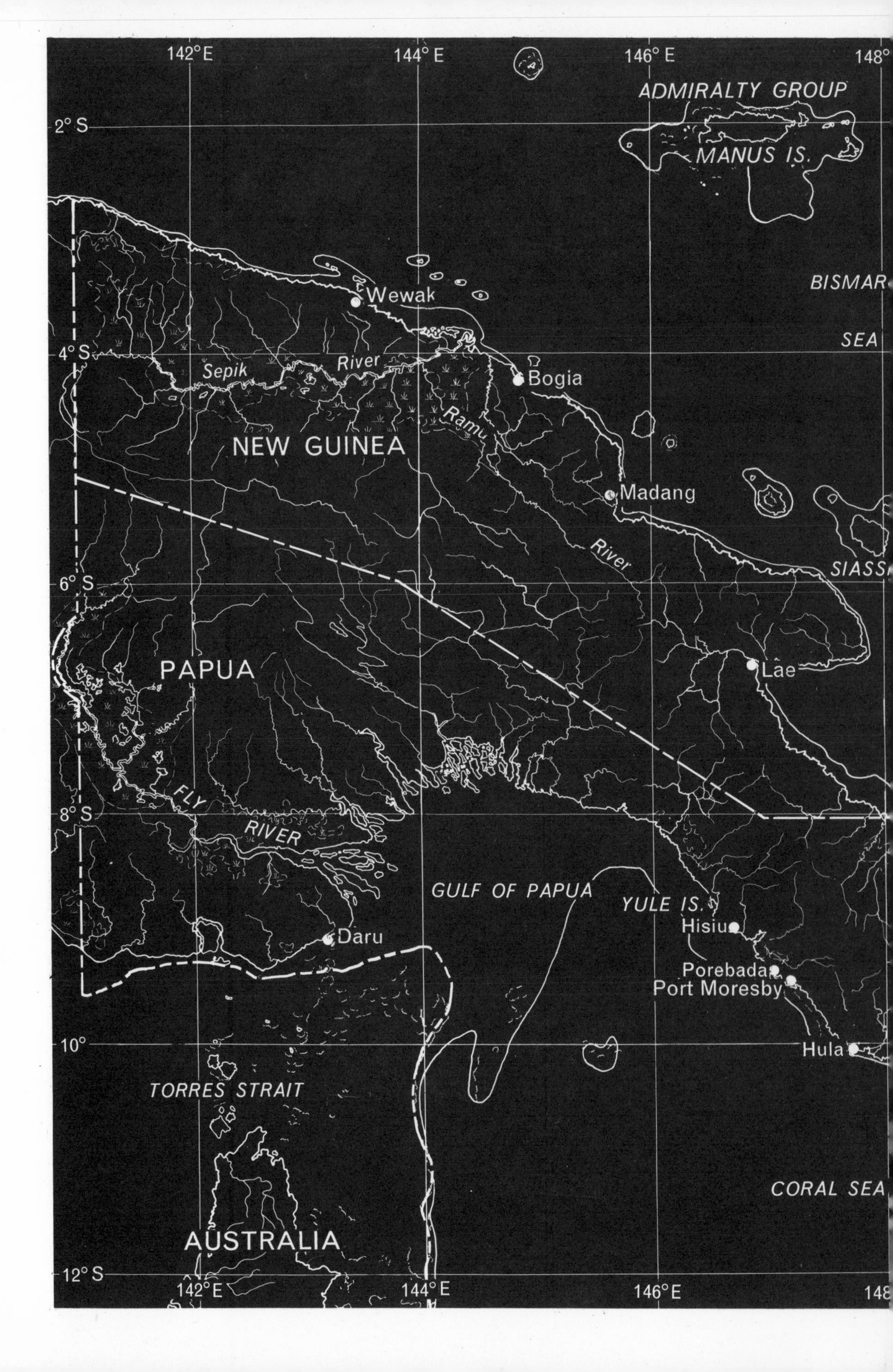
142°E
144° E
146° E
148°
ADMIRALTY GROUP
MANUS IS.
2° S
BISMAR
SEA
Wewak
4° S
Sepik
River
Bogia
Ramu
NEW GUINEA
Madang
River
6° S
SIASS
PAPUA
Lae
FLY
RIVER
8° S
GULF OF PAPUA
YULE IS.
Hisiu
Daru
Porebada
Port Moresby
10°
Hula
TORRES STRAIT
CORAL SEA
AUSTRALIA
12° S
142°E
144°E
146°E
148